Millennials
Taking the Lead

John,
   I enjoyed your
Optimist's meeting and hope
you enjoy the book.

Carolyn Fore
January 16, 2018

Millennials Taking the Lead

The Leadership Style That's Changing the Workplace

Carolyn White Fore, PhD

MOUNTAIN ARBOR PRESS

MOUNTAIN ARBOR
PRESS
Alpharetta, GA

ISBN: 978-1-63183-152-2

Library of Congress Control Number: 2017913009

10 9 8 7 6 5 4 3 2   0 9 2 3 1 7

Printed in the United States of America

♾This paper meets the requirements of ANSI/NISO Z39.48-1992 (Permanence of Paper)

Interior images by Alliene Bouchard

This book is dedicated to all the members of my family for believing in me and constantly teaching me about life. There are also a lot of wonderful friends and coworkers who have helped me understand the real-life lessons that went into writing this book, and I am very grateful to them for being part of this experience.

That which seems the height of absurdity in one generation often becomes the height of wisdom in another.

— Adlai Stevenson

Contents

Foreword

Like many Millennials, I'm a pragmatic leader with big dreams. I find it inspiring to be part of a generation that wants to help people in ways that allow us to maximize our skills. Through the interviews in this book, the reader can recognize the true heart of the Millennial leader mindset, and in doing so, better understand what drives our generation and why we do things the way we do.

This book is a valuable resource in helping today's leaders understand tomorrow's leaders. The concepts presented provide non-Millennial leaders with practical tools so they can better work with and shape aspiring Millennials as they rapidly become a dominant influence in global businesses. The reader will learn how Millennials view our own unique leadership style, and what we seek in leaders who are creating successful organizational behaviors and achievements. The dialogue captured from interviews with Millennial leaders will undoubtedly help organizational leaders improve the working relationships in a multigenerational workplace, by providing insight into the misunderstandings between Millennial leaders' expectations and those of the non-Millennial generations. By better understanding generational working relationships, leaders of all ages will be equipped with the tools to increase employee engagement, productivity, and retention rates for Millennials.

I was introduced to Carolyn through a friend several years ago, and we quickly hit it off as we learned that we had many connections through family and friends. I also learned that

Carolyn has a unique perspective on leadership from various generational perspectives and was sincerely interested in learning more about how Millennials view leadership and helping people from older generations understand their view. Her analysis of the values, beliefs, attitudes, and behaviors of leaders of different generations is enlightening for anyone who wants to understand why different generations view their work environment differently.

Carolyn is an authority on the topic of multigenerational leadership and the leadership style of Millennials through her work on her doctoral dissertation and years of experience as the leader of a multigenerational team in a corporate environment. She currently stays engaged with Millennials though teaching graduate-level business courses and networking with Millennials through volunteer work. As the parent of a Millennial leader, she has many opportunities to hear the view of this generation firsthand. She is easily accessible and always ready to discuss the challenges and solutions of the multigenerational workforce.

—Haley Kilpatrick
Founder, Girl Talk
Author, The Drama Years

Acknowledgments

I have many people to thank for helping make this book a reality. I would never have written anything without my amazing daughter, Amy, who inspired me and served as an example of an outstanding Millennial leader. She exemplifies what we have to look forward to as Millennials take on more leadership roles. Her encouragement and ability to introduce me to other Millennials who were not only willing to talk to me, but actually wanted to tell me their stories, constantly kept me going from the time I started working on this topic for my doctoral dissertation through the completion of this book. I also owe a huge debt of gratitude to another amazing Millennial leader, Amy's BFF—also known as my "other daughter," Kathy—who jumped in when I felt I needed to talk to more Millennials and introduced me to another group of outstanding Millennial leaders. While the Millennial leaders I interviewed are mostly anonymous contributors, they range from quiet leaders to some real superstars, and I thank each one for contributing their time, sharing their stories, and representing their generation.

While my Millennial leader daughter inspired and challenged me, I can't overlook the importance of the role my practical Generation X son, Will, played in helping me. He thinks I can do anything and reminded me when I needed encouragement that I always told him to strive for whatever he wanted and I should do the same. I also want to acknowledge my sincere gratitude to the rest of my family and my friends for their patience and encouragement during this long journey and for believing in me even when I did not.

Two special individuals helped me tremendously along the way. I am grateful to Bonnie Daneker of Write Advisors for her experience and insight on how to develop the material I had used for my dissertation into a book. I could not have done it without her guidance. I am also grateful to Susan Longley's great coaching for keeping me on track working toward my goals.

I also cannot help thinking how happy my parents would be if they were still here to see me reach this accomplishment. Together they instilled in me the desire to learn, achieve goals, and be a leader, making sure I had the skills I needed to be successful in life. I am forever grateful to them for their influence.

Introduction

The Millennial generation will have a marked impact on organizations as the mix of generations in the workforce changes and Millennials become prominent in the labor pool in numbers even larger than the Baby Boomers that raised them. Approximately 80 million Millennials now compete in size with approximately the same number of Baby Boomers, versus a much smaller Generation X at an estimated 46 million.[1] In the next five to fifteen years, organizations in the United States will lose between 30 and 40 percent of their current workforce. The generation identified as Traditionalists will all leave the workforce, and Baby Boomers are leaving in increasingly large numbers, with 10,000 Baby Boomers reaching age sixty-five daily.[2] Due to the decline in birth rates following the Baby Boomers, the United States faces a potential labor shortage of 35 million qualified, skilled, and educated workers for the next two to three decades.[3] Baby Boomers and Generation Xers will hold the majority of leadership positions for the next two decades, with Millennials quickly joining them to fill this gap.

This shift in generational groups affects the dynamics of the workforce. Millennials are entering the workforce during a time of increased worker diversity, a trend influenced by globalization and the presence of more women and minorities, yet generational differences are often overlooked as a diversity factor. At the same time, organizations are becoming flatter and more employee driven. As a result of these changes, leadership in organizations is transitioning from the hierarchical approach used by

Traditionalists, to a more collaborative approach preferred by Generation Xers and Millennials.

Such potent generational differences can also have a powerful impact on leaders and leadership. The common lack of clear identification and understanding of Millennials, particularly in their potential as leaders, leaves management making assumptions that, if incorrect, could negatively impact the future of their organizations.

With the exit of Traditionalist leaders from the workforce and the beginning of retirement for Baby Boomers, Generation Xers and Millennials will begin to fill more leadership positions in organizations. A better understanding of the leadership style of Millennial leaders will help organizations adapt to this group of workers in hiring, motivating, incentivizing, and retaining these valuable human assets. To realize their potential, Millennials need training, mentoring, coaching, and proper placement in their organizations. The leaders from the Millennial generational cohort will be a dominant factor in the workforce in a few years, making it crucial that today's leaders begin to understand tomorrow's leaders.

Why was I interested in the challenge?

I first recognized my interest in the relationship between leadership and generational groups as my own role as a Baby Boomer leader expanded. While developing my leadership skills through many years in the business world, I became interested in grooming new leaders. Working with employees in my own organization, and through a mentoring program in the business community, I could see how different individuals' approaches to leadership varied based on their life experiences and generational values.

I also watched my Millennial daughter develop into a strong leader, beginning in her high school years. When she advanced to a large university, she became involved in more leadership activities and was selected to be part of an elite group of students in a leadership-development program. Through observing my daughter and her friends, I began to realize that Millennial leaders had expectations and behaviors that were different from the generational groups currently in the workforce, including my own.

In addition to my Millennial daughter, I have a son and two stepchildren who are Generation Xers. Watching my children become adults, along with managing a group of generationally diverse individuals at work, was both challenging and enlightening. Observing my employees and my children as they matured and advanced in their organizations made me aware that events during the formative years of life deeply influence a person's perspective in many areas throughout his or her life. I also realized that these events create a relatable bond for the individuals within each generational cohort, just as I have with other Baby Boomers. I often hear criticism of the younger generations, especially Millennials, for not appreciating what they have, not being willing to work hard, not understanding what the older generations have done for them, and other negative sentiments. I am usually quick to defend the younger Millennial group for the positive virtues they bring to the table, and point out a few facts in their favor. Although I appreciate my life as a Baby Boomer, I find the Millennials to be a positive force with a promising future.

When my youngest child was in college, I decided it was time for me to pursue that elusive doctoral degree I had dreamed about earlier in my life. By this time, my interest had changed from my early love for chemistry and computers to my fascination for developing leaders and dissecting organizational culture. The result was my completion of a doctor of philosophy in organization and management from Capella University and my dissertation topic, "Next Generation Leadership: Millennials as Leaders." The interviews with Millennial leaders, the research for my dissertation, and the many papers I wrote while completing my degree are the foundation of this book.

My purpose in writing this book is to help today's leaders begin to understand tomorrow's leaders in three ways: to describe how Millennials view their own unique leadership style, to illustrate what Millennials look for in leaders creating successful organizational behaviors and achievements, and to provide today's leaders with more practical tools so they can better work with and shape aspiring Millennials as they are rapidly becoming a dominant influence in the global businesses of the future.

What I learned about the leadership style of Millennials from my dissertation research is illustrated in the themes that emerged from my interviews with Millennial leaders to capture their views of their own generation's leadership style. The characteristics that any generational cohort brings to the workplace are a result of the values, beliefs, preferences, and attitudes formed earlier in their lives. This fact is exemplified in the leadership characteristics that are most important to Millennial leaders.

Why should you be interested in the results?

The lack of understanding of generational differences is creating conflict in the workplace. By understanding the different generational perspectives of team members, particularly within the leadership teams, an organizational leader can more effectively take steps to prevent or minimize such conflicts.

Two groups of individuals will likely be most interested in reading this book. The primary audience is the management in the organizations where Millennials are now working or will be working.

There often appears to be a significant amount of misunderstanding and doubt from current management regarding our younger team members. I would like to help current leaders better understand Millennials and what approaches are best for helping cultivate these young potential leaders into greatness.

The questioning leaders of today must recognize that developing new talent is essential to companies in preventing a serious lack of skilled leadership in a few short years.

The other party expressing an interest in the content of this book consists of aspiring Millennials who want to be heard. I have listened to a representative group of Millennial leaders describe their leadership style, and one of the things I consistently heard them talk about was their need for a voice in the workplace. They are anxious to have someone outside of their generation understand their perspective and represent them within their organizations' currently established leadership.

How will this book help you?

This book clarifies many of the misunderstandings about Millennials as leaders, and in doing so provides information that helps their employers see the potential of new, outstanding talent within their teams. At the same time, the Millennials who read the book will, hopefully, have a better understanding of why they are misunderstood and gather some helpful hints on how to work more cohesively with the older generations in the workplace. It may be hard to recognize at this point that Millennials will one day be the older generation facing similar issues as future generations enter the workforce. However, it is in everyone's best interest to start understanding how our differences shape our views, as well as new ways of learning to work together to bridge those gigantic generational gaps.

Chapter 1

Millennials as Leaders

As leaders of organizations retire and more members of younger generations move into leadership roles, their inherent generational differences—a result of their different perspectives on leadership—will change the type of leadership emerging in organizations. Each generation comes to the workforce with its own set of beliefs, values, preferences, and attitudes, and therefore imposes its specific influence on the organization. As a result, future leaders are likely to exhibit characteristics consistent with their beliefs, values, preferences, and attitudes that differ from those of previous generations due to their respective life experiences. For example, members of older generations tend to view leadership as an authoritative role, whereas members of younger generations tend to view leadership more as an earned role based on competency. With the new dynamic of four generations in the workforce, organizations face both opportunities and challenges in adapting to the influx of a new generation of leaders. The different mixes in age, gender, race, and geography further complicate changing workforce demographics.

Millennials—Americans born between 1980 and 2000—are entering the workforce as the most optimistic, educated generational cohort group in US history, already taking many organizations by surprise as employers look for ways to attract and retain this talent pool. These individuals, who have become accustomed to stepping up to leadership positions in school, volunteer organizations, and part-time jobs, enter the workforce with high expectations and a desire to make a difference. Yet the current members of the organizations into which these young people are stepping are questioning these newcomers as future leaders and how they fit into the leadership roles to which they aspire. As mentioned in the introduction, the lack of understanding of generational differences is also creating conflict in the workplace. By better understanding these differences, especially in the leadership teams, today's leaders can take steps to prevent or minimize generational conflict in their organizations.

What are the different generations and their leadership styles?

The *generational cohort* is not a new concept, but it has become a more popular area of study in recent years because humans are living longer. Each age group, or cohort, has its personality, influenced by events that occurred during those individuals' developmental years. As each group reached certain ages, the characteristics of that group influenced their actions. Well-known authors William Strauss and Neil Howe proposed that the lifestyles of future generations could be predicted based on observing the cycles of past and current generations.[1] The social aspects of how generational groups get along with each other in society became a predominant theme in generational cohort literature as people began to live longer and became more aware of generational differences.

Recent research focus on generational differences in the workforce is the result of the Millennial cohort's entry into the workforce over the past ten years. This created the first time in American history with four distinct generations in the workforce. There are differing views on the exact breakdown and naming conventions of the generational cohorts. I use what appears to be the most frequently used convention in defining the generations as the following:

Traditionalists (born 1925–1945)
Baby Boomers (born 1946–1964)
Generation X (born 1965–1979)
Millennials (born 1980–2000)

Each generation has different goals and styles. As one popular book describes it, these four generations have "unique work ethics, different perspectives on work, distinct and preferred ways of managing and being managed, idiosyncratic styles, and unique ways of viewing such work-world issues as quality, service, and well . . . just showing up for work."[2]

Differences in the beliefs, values, preferences, and attitudes of each generation affect how each generation views leadership. Thus, generational leadership changes affect organizations. Currently, for instance, with Traditionalists almost completely out of the workforce and Baby Boomers retiring at increasing rates, opportunities for Generation Xers and Millennials to move into leadership positions are being created at an accelerating pace. As generational shifts take place in the workforce, the attitudes of the individuals in the workforce change, the expectations of leaders change, and the leaders themselves change. Generational research records recent changes in the workforce as organizations shift from primarily rank and hierarchy structures to flatter, global organizations with more employee decision making. Changes in leadership styles reflect the generational shift in values from Traditionalists' and Baby Boomers' loyalty to the organization and desire to succeed, to Generation Xers' and Millennials' expectation of stimulation, feedback, and free agency.

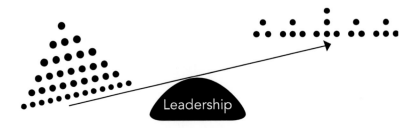

Leadership style is the preferred method of influencing others toward accomplishing goals. Descriptions of leadership style include terms such as *autocratic, charismatic, democratic* or *participatory, laissez-faire, servant,* and/or *transformational. Situational leadership* refers to the use of several styles at different times, invoked by a leader based on the specific situation.₃ Regardless of the leadership style, leaders must engage and inspire those they lead and serve, thus creating an organizational culture and climate that promotes teamwork and collaboration amid the challenges and opportunities of the multigenerational workforce in organizations.

What is known about the relationship between generational groups and leadership?

Research studies on generational trends in the workforce most often look at issues related to the Traditionalist generation leaving the workforce, Baby Boomers beginning to retire, Generation Xers looking for their role, and Millennials entering the workforce in large numbers with high expectations and excellent educations. Research between generations compares worker motivation, job satisfaction, job commitment, and leadership preferences.

Studies on *leadership preferences* by generation show differences in the type of leadership preferred by the different generational cohorts based on their values:

Traditionalists	prefer leaders who are direct, take charge, and make unilateral decisions.
Baby Boomers	prefer leaders who are participatory, collegial, and consensual.
Generation Xers	challenge authority and look for their leaders to demonstrate their competence, adapt to change, and be fair, participatory, and diversity-sensitive.
Millennials	look for leaders to provide guidance, exhibit competence, develop strong interpersonal relationships, foster a positive work environment, be able to self-manage, and possess excellent communication skills.

Awareness of this unprecedented multigenerational workforce has sparked interest in how Millennials behave in the work environment and interact with other generational groups. Millennials have started their jobs as the most optimistic, eager, enthusiastic employees to enter the workforce. They are graduating from college in large numbers each year as the best-educated generation, with résumés listing part-time jobs, internships, community-service work, and leadership positions in school organizations. They are ambitious, having grown up in a child-centered environment, at home in a world dominated by technology and instant gratification, influenced by their Baby Boomer parents. They are willing to work hard, yet expect immediate gratification and quick advancement in return.

This lack of understanding of how Millennials perceive themselves as leaders and their leadership style has made it difficult to develop leadership programs that address the type of leadership Millennials are looking for, and even more difficult to mentor and provide ongoing training for this group. Research shows that the way leaders identify and describe themselves is a predictor of their desired leadership development. For this reason, self-identification and self- description are valid methods of collecting the information needed to better understand the leadership style of Millennials.

Research in recent generational cohort literature documents specific leadership styles for each of the three older generational cohorts currently in the workforce. The material for this book is based on my research study that used generational theory and leadership theory to explore how Millennials describe their generational cohort's leadership style.

What is the recent information on Millennial leaders?

There is an organizational impact of generational-cohort differences on leaders and leadership. The current lack of identification and understanding of Millennials as leaders leaves management making assumptions that, if incorrect, could impact the future of their organizations.

Most Traditionalist leaders have already retired, and each year sees more Baby Boomer leaders reaching retirement age, leaving Generation Xers and Millennials to fill more leadership positions in organizations. Successful organizations will need to begin understanding the leadership style of Millennial leaders in order to hire, motivate, and retain these future leaders. The leaders from the Millennial generational cohort will soon be a dominant factor in the workforce, making it important that today's leaders begin to understand tomorrow's leaders.

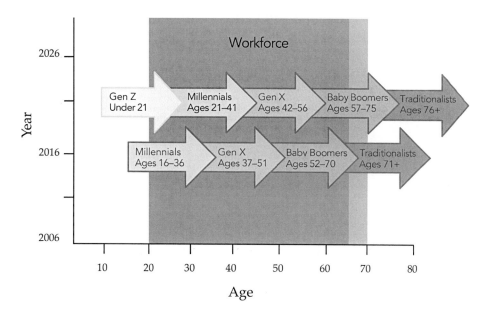

As previously mentioned, identified differences in leadership styles of the generational cohorts impact organizations as leaders of older generations begin to retire. The leadership styles of Traditionalists, Baby Boomers, and Generation Xers have been described in the literature on generational differences, yet the leadership style of the newest group of leaders, Millennials, is only beginning to be addressed due to their recent entry into leadership positions. Therefore, research was needed to describe the leadership style of Millennial leaders.

What were my study and my findings?

To address the need for research on the leadership style of Millennial leaders, I conducted a study for my doctoral dissertation to explore the topic. The study addressed one central research question: *What are Millennial leaders' leadership styles as described by Millennial leaders?* I asked a number of additional questions that were implicit in the research question to help clarify and explore how Millennials describe their generational cohort's leadership style, including the following:

- What are Millennial leaders' definitions of leadership?
- What are Millennial leaders' preferences in and expectations of a leader or role model as a leader?
- What are Millennial leaders' descriptions of how their followers would describe Millennials' leadership style?
- What are Millennial leaders' beliefs, values, preferences, and attitudes as leaders?
- What are Millennial leaders' influences in their personal leadership development?
- What are Millennial leaders' visions of their preferred leadership style?

Current organizational leaders and workers from other generational cohorts do not know what to expect from Millennials as they move into leadership roles. Obtaining information on how Millennials lead others benefits organizations and their current leaders by helping determine how these Millennial leaders will align with existing organizational leaders from other generational groups with potentially different leadership styles.

The findings of this research can also assist in determining the types of coaching, training, mentoring, and leadership development needed by Millennial leaders. Having more information about Millennial leaders assists organizations in creating leadership-development programs designed specifically for the next generation of leaders. The information obtained through the research benefits Millennial leaders as they seek mentoring and guidance to assist them in their growth toward becoming future leaders. This is accomplished by providing a better understanding of Millennial leaders' beliefs, values, preferences, and expectations in leadership roles.

In addition, insight into the younger generation of leaders who will influence organizations in the future helps organizations leverage generational differences for increased effectiveness and business performance through improved teamwork and knowledge transfer. Organizations should begin planning for the upcoming need to fill the large number of vacancies that will be created as Baby Boomer leaders continue to retire. In order for organizations to be prepared, they will have to compete for the best workers in the Millennial cohort, the newest group entering the workforce. They will also need to begin to transition leadership positions to this next generation.

Who were the study participants?

Study participants were interviewed to explore their descriptions of the Millennial cohort's leadership style and to gather additional information about Millennials' views of leadership and their own leadership development. The ages of participants ranged from twenty-three to thirty-five at the time they were interviewed, with birth years from 1980 to 1989 (see Appendix). The first group of participants was interviewed for my dissertation, then a second group was interviewed later to have more data for this book. The organizations selected to solicit participants have ethnically diverse populations. All participants were raised in the United States in various parts of the country, although the majority of the participants lived in one of the Southern states all or some of the years between ages of five and eighteen.

Participants worked for a variety of employers. In order to ensure anonymity, the employers have been grouped into general types rather than specific categories: business services, education services, financial/real estate, government, management-consulting services, marketing/advertising, media, and nonprofit. Because some participants had unique job titles, participants' positions have also been grouped into categories to indicate their level of responsibility within their organization, as either a project manager/team-lead leadership role or executive/management leadership role. Pseudonyms were assigned to each participant by randomly selecting a name from the most popular baby names for each gender from the year 1984, the midpoint for participants' birth years, ensuring that none of the names randomly selected matched any of the participants' names.[4]

All study participants appeared very willing to be open and honest in their responses. All shared their personal experiences and their views of Millennials as leaders, while expressing interest in representing their generational cohort to let others know more about their perspectives on leadership. The responses to some interview questions were similar across the group of participants; for other interview questions the responses were more varied, as discussed in the following chapters.

What themes evolved from the research data?

Ten key themes evolved from analysis of the data, related to leaders' *passion, trust, social consciousness, doing the right thing, collaboration, technology, mentoring, doing what they say they'll do, work-life balance,* and *continuous learning.* These themes will be discussed in detail in the following chapters, including comments from the interviews.

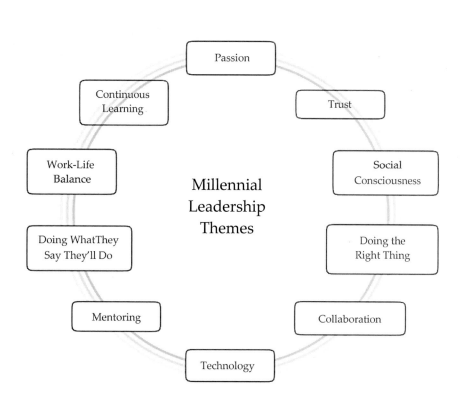

Passion

Trust

Continuous
Learning

Social
Consciousness

Work-Life
Balance

Millennial
Leadership
Themes

Doing WhatThey
Say They'll Do

Doing the
Right Thing

Mentoring

Collaboration

Technology

Visual Indicators You Will Find in This Book

 Passion

 ContinuousLearning

 Work-Life Balance

 Doing What They Say They'll Do

 Mentoring

 Technology

 Collaboration

 Doing the Right Thing

 Social Consciousness

 Trust

Chapter 2

Leaders Have Passion

Imba Means Sing

One of the most passionate Millennial leaders I know gave up her job to pursue her passion. Erin had discovered her passion for helping others early in life. She developed her talent for storytelling through the media, and her ability for fundraising through volunteer activities in high school and college. She worked with a local television station during high school, and after college Erin landed a job in cable television. She intensified her fundraising activities when she raised over a million dollars for nonprofit programs she felt inspired to support. While in Africa, Erin met and fell in love with the young children in the African Children's Choir who had so much talent and hope for a path to a better future. After working for cable news for several years, Erin decided it was time to put her passion into telling the story of the African Children's Choir. She left her secure job and traveled with them for a year working on a documentary telling their story as a fundraiser for the choir.

But first she had to raise funds to cover the expense to create the film. She could not have done this without her talent and the experience she had gained from her previous work; however, her passion was the real driving force that kept her going. The film, *Imba Means Sing*, takes viewers into the lives and dreams of these African children.

As I started my interview with the third Millennial leader in my study, I became acutely aware of how passionately he spoke about many of the ideas he had about leadership. I immediately thought about the previous interviews and recalled that same expression of passion. After we finished the interview, I couldn't stop thinking about how quickly that had become a theme among these Millennial leaders, and I wondered if it would continue. As I transcribed the rest of the interviews, I heard them use the word *passion* in their comments and listened for that excited tone in their voices. It was definitely there.

Whether leading or observing other leaders, Millennial leaders believe that passion is the driving force that motivates individuals or groups. Leaders of all ages talk about the need to find their passion. This is extremely important to Millennial leaders. When interviewing Millennial leaders, the words *passion* and *dedication* combined with the enthusiasm they exhibited when discussing their ideas was apparent to me immediately because they frequently used these words when discussing leaders or leadership. Comments about passion indicated that it would be difficult to lead without a passion for the purpose, goal, or vision that was to be accomplished. These Millennial leaders also stated that whether leading or observing other leaders, passion motivated others when working as individuals or in groups. The following summarizes their views on passion and leadership:

- Millennial leaders feel passion drives leaders.
- Leaders must be passionate to inspire others to follow them.
- Millennial leaders want to feel passionate about the organizations in which they are leading others.

What does passion look like?

Millennial leaders believe that great leadership skills are discovered when an individual is placed in a situation they are passionate about, and that is often when they discover their leadership abilities. These leaders recognize there is nothing like "sink or swim" to make them realize they have to step up to their true leadership potential. They realize that sometimes they don't recognize their own leadership capabilities until after the crisis or situation is over, but looking back they may understand what a leadership-growth opportunity it was. As leaders, they acknowledge that if they had not been passionate about what they believed in, they probably would not have been successful in the outcome.

Many of these Millennial leaders commented that it was difficult to be a great leader without a passion for the purpose, vision, or goal that needed to be accomplished. Michael described a leader as "someone who has got to have passion, *strong* passion, for whatever they are doing." From her perspective as a leader, Amanda stated, "I'm going to take the lead because I'm passionate about getting things done." When Heather described leaders she said, "It's always interesting to me to be around people who are passionate about one thing and that drives them to be a leader."

You can't give another person passion. What you can do is take away roadblocks that keep them from being passionate about something they already feel passionate about. As a good leader, you can help another person find ways to express their passion and inspire them to pursue their interests in this area. A good leader can also connect passionate people who have the same goals, and help them direct their passion toward achievements and accomplishments that will make them feel proud. As Amanda shared in describing a leader she had worked for who had inspired her, "[The president of the company] basically talked about how we need to find our passion. That's a big thing for my generation."

The general feeling among the Millennial leaders was that it could be difficult to lead others if you don't have the passion it takes to inspire others to see and feel your vision. For that reason, Millennial leaders felt that to be good leaders, they needed to have that same kind of passion they saw in the leaders who inspired them. According to Jessica, "Great, quality leadership skills develop when you are put in a situation or in a work environment you are passionate about, and then the true leader emerges."

Nicole also felt strongly about passion as she stated, "I think what really elevates someone to the next level—this is just really hard to put into words—the passion, I think, passion and vision. You have these ground workings, that's fabulous. You have to have these concrete, solid ideas of where you want to go, and you have to be passionate about it." This statement acknowledges the recognition that in addition to passion to inspire others, a good leader needs a vision and a goal to accomplish.

Rachel said, "That's fundamentally what I think is really important about a leader—that you can inspire others. And you can't inspire others if you aren't passionate. Behind every leader is a passion." Michael commented, "I try to lead by example. I also try to give people on my team at work as much autonomy as I can. And it's interesting because I struggle a little bit when people actually ask for very specific direction."

Millennials have gained a reputation for not being able to do things for themselves, primarily because they have received a lot of direction and support all their lives. As working adults, most of them like to figure things out for themselves, but expect to be given some direction and to have someone to go to when they need assistance. As leaders, they don't want to provide a lot of direction, just the goals and key expectations, but will be available for assistance if needed. They are counting on their passion and enthusiasm energizing the personal efforts of their team. This fits with their view of leadership as guiding others toward the shared goal by inspiring others through the dedication and passion the leader exhibits.

Millennial leaders translate their passion for inspiring others to their passion for their organizations. It's important that they feel some passion for the organization in some way. As Elizabeth described it, "I don't lead anything that I don't care about. And, obviously, I don't think you should be a leader unless you are really passionate about the organization." There are a lot of ways to be passionate about your organization. It may be the people, the values, the vision, the goals, or something about the organization that you identify with. Danielle described her view of the importance of sharing a passion for the goals when she stated, "The leader I respected most was passionate about the goals of the organization, and made those goals feel important to me through her passion."

When describing their leadership styles, participants discussed passion, motivating and inspiring others, and building relationships. Participants discussed the importance of passion giving them the drive to want to lead others. As described by Joshua, "As a leader I'm passionate. I like to be seen as someone who cares about the people I'm leading." The passionate, selfless, and collaborative nature of these Millennial leaders defines them and gives them their unique style. Millennial leaders are passionate about their work, but they are also passionate about their friends, their families, and their volunteer activities.

 "I don't lead anything that I don't care about. And, obviously, I don't think you should be a leader unless you are really passionate about the organization."

How does passion fit in the workplace today?

The leadership style of Millennials fits with the emerging need of organizations to have leadership that connects, collaborates, and is driven by passion and purpose to provide the organization with a common cause. Millennials often leave their jobs because they feel they are not given the opportunity to be heard or to contribute. A large part of this is related to their passion. They feel passionately about how they can contribute to a project or their insight as a young person who empathizes and understands the trends of their age group. Often they encounter the discouraging response of being shut down in a meeting or their manager telling them, individually, that they don't have enough experience to contribute. They are often informed they should listen and learn in these situations. As a result, the Millennials may have some great ideas that aren't heard. By not allowing Millennials to contribute, current leaders are missing the opportunity to learn from this generation about how to tap into their peers. If the approach of the individual wasn't appropriate due to their lack of experience, then it can be a teaching and mentoring opportunity to help that individual with their communication skills. What frequently happens, instead, is that their entire message is lost, leaving the project or the company without information that could be valuable. It also creates an unhappy Millennial employee who will likely leave the organization after a few of these experiences.

The passion and optimism of Millennials can be refreshing and rewarding when an organization appreciates the value of new ideas and the benefits a positive attitude can bring to their environment. The creativity gained by looking at the work with a new perspective can lead to new, often more efficient, ways to accomplish the work. Millennials often bring an alternate view that can either lead them to recommend a new way to do the job, or spark an idea for someone who knows the current process to look at it differently and improve the process.

A winning situation occurs when an organization's leaders have directed the passion of their Millennials toward furthering the goals of the organization, whether it is the long-term objectives or short-term goals of the organization's projects. Using the creativity and enthusiasm of this generation will likely be beneficial to the outcome and engaging to the individuals.

When a Millennial is passionate about an idea, put that passion to work. Whenever there is a way that allows them to work in the area they are passionate about, the results will be much better. If it isn't possible to let them do exactly what they want, try to channel that passion into the area that is the best match. It will be rewarding for both the individual and the organization.

Takeaways

Millennial leaders want to see passion in the leaders they follow. They will be more inspired and engaged in the organization if they feel their leaders are passionate about the goals. They will then follow that passion and do their best to help attain the goals for this type of leader.

Millennial leaders need to feel passion to be committed to what they are doing. They are dedicated to accomplishing goals when they believe in them and are enthusiastic about the work. Without a passion for the work they are doing, Millennial leaders will not stay involved and will not inspire others to be involved. They recognize that in addition to passion to inspire others, a good leader needs a vision and a goal to accomplish. Without constantly feeding passion, a leader loses the momentum and the ability to focus on the goals. When there's no passion, there are no followers. Current leaders should take advantage of the Millennials' passion and direct it in ways that positively affect them and the culture of the organization.

Not only are Millennials inspired by passion and want the ability to express it, they are also collaborative and communicate often with their peers. When they are inspired and passionate about their work or volunteer activities, they let others know about it.

If you have Millennials working for you, recognize and acknowledge their passion and put it to work. Show your passion as a leader if you expect them to get behind your efforts. The same thing applies to the organization and how it portrays its vision and goals. If the Millennial leaders feel there is a passion for the work the organization is doing, they will be more committed to the organization.

* * * * *

Leadership is inspired by passion in the view of the Millennial leaders. A leader inspires people to act. A leader's team trusts the leader enough to want to follow along or work together to accomplish the vision or goal. Millennials mentioned trust frequently and emphatically in the interviews, and mutual trust is critical for Millennial leaders and their employers.

Chapter 3

Trust

Give Me a Chance to Try

When you asked me about a perfect leader, I thought of my boss as an amazing example. She gives me rope to hang myself. She says, "I'll support you. If you go forward and you try something, if you don't actually try to hurt anybody and you don't steal, or lie, or cheat, and it goes wrong, I'll still support you." I have all this freedom and I think that's a really important part of being a leader. You have to find these people to follow you and work with you, and you can't micromanage what they do. You have to trust them enough to give them leeway to try things and risk failing, because if you don't, you're not going to get anything cool done. You have to risk bad things happening to be able to achieve something. So the "rope to hang yourself" is the way I look at it. I can either achieve something when I can take this on and step up to the challenge, or I can falter. That's worked really well for me. I love that environment.

—*Quote from a Millennial leader*

Millennial leaders stated that both trust and honesty are essential parts of leadership. Millennial leaders wanted to have confidence in the sincerity of the relationship and the authenticity of the leader. If a person in a leadership role could not be trusted, he or she would not maintain the support of his or her followers for long and, consequently, would not be able to accomplish his or her goals. Participants also indicated that the relationship of trust must be reciprocal because leaders need to know they can trust their followers and count on them for their support.

Credibility is the foundation of effective leadership; people want leaders who are honest, forward looking, competent, and inspiring.[1] Leadership is a process by which an individual influences others to accomplish a stated objective, while directing the organization in a more cohesive and coherent way. Leaders accomplish this by applying leadership attributes, such as visioning, personal mastery, self-awareness, interpersonal skills, encouraging the heart, knowledge and skills, positive emotions, creating followership, and stewardship.[2] Nevertheless, when people are deciding if they respect a person as a leader, they don't think about the leader's attributes. They are more likely to observe a person's actions to learn who that person really is. An individual uses observation to tell if a person is an honorable and trusted leader or a self-serving person who misuses authority to look good and gain promotion.[3] Self-serving leaders are not as effective because their employees do not respect them and will merely obey them, rather than follow them.[4] Good leadership is based on honorable character and selfless service to one's organization.[5]

Each generation applies fundamental characteristics of leadership, such as honesty, in their own unique way. The Millennial generation has a reputation for being open, self-assured, hopeful, well educated, and goal oriented.[6] Millennials have benefited from each of the three older generations, receiving allegiance and trust in organizations from Traditionalists, confidence and optimism from Baby Boomers, and a healthy dose of skepticism from Generation X.[7] Millennials refocused the allegiance and trust in organizations they learned from Traditionalists to allegiance and trust in relationships. The confidence and optimism they learned from Baby Boomers helped Millennials turn the skepticism they learned from Generation X into an ability to look at the present more realistically than Baby Boomers, while still maintaining a positive outlook about the future.[8]

Is trust the ubiquitous element?

The Millennial leaders interviewed stressed the importance of trust and honesty to leadership as illustrated in their comments. According to Nicole, "You can't follow somebody or even be inspired by somebody you don't trust. You just can't." It was evident that, for Millennials, it would be hard to work for someone they didn't trust, and they certainly would not consider the person a leader. Loss of trust could permanently damage the relationship, as illustrated in Michael's comment, "If [leaders] do something that damages that trust you put in them, then it's over. It's very, very hard to get it back."

According to Nicole, "Leadership is about trust and inspiration. You have to inspire people to do something, and they have to trust that you have a vision and it's the right thing to do." She further described her work environment, saying, "We operate in a really open environment, and when you operate like that, I can't just tell somebody to go get this done or you have to do something because I said so. I have to actually inspire them to want to do it. They have to trust that I'm not leading them astray, that I have a vision."

It was equally important to Millennial leaders that they earn others' trust. As Melissa stated, "I want people to trust me. I feel like I'm a pretty trustworthy person and pretty honest. I think when you trust somebody, you are far more likely to do things for them and do things in a positive way." Amanda recognized that trust was *earned* rather than *assumed*, and talked about the advice she received from a manager regarding trust: "He just looked at me and said, 'You have to build clout sometimes, and whether that's right or wrong, it's true. As human beings, it takes time to build trust.'"

"You can't follow somebody or even be inspired by somebody you don't trust. You just can't."

Jessica learned about trust from some negative examples in the workplace. "I learned I didn't want to be that way . . . cynical and not trusting. It may be easier to be that way, but I prefer to be naïve and believe the good in people." Michael saw both sides of this in his work environment. "Once [my manager] recognized that I was trying hard and I was capable, trust developed. Trust in the team and the people around you. I had the best intentions and [my employees] were trying really hard. Some leaders don't believe in that. They are always second-guessing their own team. That doesn't really work for me."

When Sarah described a leader she admired, she said, "He is very clear about the goals that he wants to achieve and I think he's very good about motivating people and making them feel valued. But he's not a micromanager and he's very hands off. He puts a lot of trust in people beneath him and expects that they will live up to his expectations."

Honesty may be more important than ever in today's world of social media and increased speed and breadth of communications. If a leader is not transparent and honest, this is likely to be discovered in a short amount of time and certainly does not seem worth the consequences. According to Danielle, "A Millennial leader is not going to trust or want to work with a leader who has demonstrated lack of honesty or transparency."

"If [leaders] do something that
damages that trust you put in
them, then it's over.
It's very, very hard to get it back."

This transparency leads to an understanding of the reasons behind the actions, and it needs to be for the right motivation, or once again, the trust will be lost. As Brandon experienced, "There have been many times in my life where I put trust in people who were leading aspects of my thoughts for particular topics where they were not doing it for the right reasons, they were not doing as they said, they were not taking action upon opinion, and at the end of the day, things fell apart in materially negative ways because of that. And so I learned from that."

Millennial leaders in this study illustrated the importance of values to leadership in their discussions of trust, good moral values, doing what is right, and honesty. Prior research indicates that each of the four generations currently in the workforce believes that honesty is an important characteristic for leaders.[9] However, they may not view these values with the same priority or perspective. Millennials are often concerned about looking out for others and doing what is good for everyone.

Generational Perspectives
on Trust in the Workplace

Generation	View of Trust as It Relates to Work
Traditionalists (1925–1945)	Allegiance to the organization
Baby Boomers (1946–1964)	Teamwork; trusting others to accomplish the goals together
Generation X (1965–1979)	Skepticism; who do I trust?
Millennials (1980–2000)	Working together for the greater good; transparency

How do you instill trust?

Millennial leaders need to feel that they can trust their mentors, leaders, and the organizations to which they belong. Their strong moral values provide the basis for their trust in others, the importance of honesty, their desire to do the right thing, and their reasons for caring about others. Millennial leaders will continue to work only with companies where they feel valued and sense that there is trust, honesty, and transparency. These are major components of recruiting and grooming the talent for your organization. To give them opportunities to earn your trust and develop into their leadership potential, give them projects that will stretch them.

Inspiring Millennial leaders to believe in the vision and goals of the organization requires a sense of trust that the organization's leaders are being transparent and honest in sharing the information needed to attain the goals. Millennials want to know as much as possible, and may even have difficulty understanding the concept of "need-to-know only" projects and people. If there are such situations, most Millennials would want to understand why there were such limitations and for how long. Those managing Millennials should adopt a personal policy of explaining "why."

It is important to show your trust in the Millennial leaders in your organization and let them know they can trust you. As an organizational leader, you must be someone they can trust, or you are not the right leader for them. In return, learning to trust Millennials may seem more difficult, and if it is a challenge, then start with one or two areas and build that level of trust until you recognize the level of trust you are comfortable with. It is likely to provide significant positive payback.

Honesty and transparency are also essential to the relationship with Millennials and building an environment of trust in the organization. It is better to let them know what part of a project you are assigning to them and why, and that if they do well they will be given more responsibility next time. If you do that, but decide to keep that information to yourself as if it is a secret test, they will figure it out and always question your motives, never fully trusting you. The result will be that you will never have that sense of mutual trust that is needed for a good working relationship.

Takeaways

Millennials are often concerned about looking out for others and doing what is good for everyone. Millennial leaders in this study illustrated the importance of values to leadership in their discussions of trust, good moral values, and honesty. As mentioned previously, each of the four generations currently in the workforce believes that honesty is an important characteristic for leaders, but may not view these values with the same priority or perspective.

As an essential characteristic of leadership, there are three components of trust in the view of the Millennial leader:

1. The organization's vision should be trustworthy for all involved, i.e., for the greater good.
2. Leadership is honest, transparent, and can be trusted.
3. Millennials are competent and can be trusted.

Millennials expect a lot of communications and feedback. Those in leadership roles want to know even more about their own performance, their team's performance, and the company's. Some recommendations for feedback include:

- Updates on the vision and goals and how it relates to their role
- Status of their projects, including feedback on project success
- Individual feedback, with more responsibility after action or success

Many of the study participants commented on the role of a coach or other role model in encouraging them to step into a leadership role, or to recognize they were viewed as a leader and embrace it. An additional aspect of the coach as a leadership influence is the disillusionment of learning, as these Millennial leaders have become adult leaders, that not all coaches are good, honest, and trustworthy, especially in the aftermath of the Penn State case involving football coach Jerry Sandusky.

The strong moral values of these Millennial leaders provide the basis for their trust in others, the importance of honesty, their desire to do the right thing, and their reasons for caring about others. Millennial leaders will continue to work only with companies where they feel valued, sense that there is honesty and trust, and note that social responsibility is one of the goals.

* * * * *

Millennial leaders are passionate about their work and value trust in their leaders, and it is important to recognize that they carry these same values over to their friends, their families, and their volunteer activities. Social consciousness is an important part of their professional and personal lives as they learn to work with their leaders and look at the greater good.

Chapter 4

Social Consciousness

#SNOWJAM2014

Atlanta had one of its historic ice- and snowstorms the last week of January 2014. Snow in Atlanta is unusual, and traffic jams of major proportions can happen as a result of any number of events: the beginning of a holiday weekend, heavy rain, an airplane landing on a highway, or anything else that interrupts the fragile balance of traffic flow. The day of the snowstorm, everyone was trying to go home early to avoid icy roads. The massive volume of cars and trucks on iced-over roads resulted in stranded motorists who tried desperately to get home. Some made it after harrowing hours on the roads, while others took refuge in their cars or in unexpected places, like churches and grocery stores.

Many people helped others out of situations that ranged from frustrating to life threatening. While these good Samaritans were not limited to Millennials, one group of Millennial leaders, who had all made it home to warm, safe places during the snowy hours the traffic was building, stands out. They realized the next morning that there were people stranded in their cars on the interstate highways who had been there all night and were cold and hungry. Together, this group shopped for water and granola bars, then walked along the highway for hours, from one stranded car to the next, knocking on windows to see who was inside needing water, food, or assistance. They did this because they knew people needed help and they cared about helping others, all without any expected payback.

Millennial leaders often describe leaders as individuals who care about others and give back to their community, and say that leadership is about others and the greater good, not personal interests. The terms *selfless* and *servant leader* are often mentioned by Millennials when they talk about leaders they admire. Related concepts that a leader should be developing others, putting the interests of others before the leader's own interests, and helping others are similar phrases these leaders use when discussing their views on leadership.

Millennial leaders interviewed for the study admired leaders who had social interests and respect for others, more so than those who were successful for what they had accomplished. Different aspects of social consciousness that were important to participants included:

- Volunteerism on a local level
- Global efforts for fundraising and volunteerism
- Mentoring youth
- Servant leadership
- Developing young leaders

How do Millennials view leadership as helping others?

The importance of social consciousness and community was illustrated in the comments made by the Millennial leaders in the interviews. In Millennial leader Jessica's view, "Our generation has been exposed to global needs because of technology, and we are more heart driven than paycheck driven. I think that a lot that's happened since 2008 (the outset of the recession), as well as with the shifts in the economy and people kind of going back to the basics, has been a beautiful thing for our generation . . . to see our parents do that, because most of our parents lived in such excess and it was about things and money and power." Jessica's assessment was that this materialistic shift presented an opportunity for people to look at their values and what it means to help others.

Millennial leaders recognize that in the corporate world, not all companies have the same values they have, so they appreciate finding a company or a boss who makes time for volunteering and allows them to do the same. According to Rachel, "Being awake and seeing that there is a need somewhere" in the community and volunteering to help those in need is an important quality for a leader. These Millennial leaders admired leaders who took social responsibility, and respected them more than those leaders who were successful only for what they had accomplished. Leadership is about others and the greater good, not personal interests, in the view of Millennial leaders. The Millennial leaders interviewed for this study were aware of ensuring that their personal time and their organizations' resources gave a fair share to volunteer efforts and serving their community—locally or globally.

Joshua respected the leadership qualities of a leader he admired because "he was both a leader in a company and he took that success and passed it on . . . really created the new Millennial young leaders of today. He was a servant leader in that he was a leader in business, but it was important for him to translate that leadership into serving others."

In Elizabeth's view, a leader is someone who works hard for social justice. At the same time, Jessica stated that the Millennial generation is "so fueled by passion and helping others that, contrary to popular belief, we are a generation of people who want to contribute and give back." In turn, they want and expect their managers to give back.

"Our generation has been exposed to global needs because of technology, and we are more heart driven than paycheck driven."

Millennial leaders admired role models who most exemplified the behaviors they wanted to exhibit as leaders. These role models were selfless leaders who demonstrated a desire to help others and mentor or teach them to also become good leaders. In addition, participants indicated they preferred leaders and role models who exhibit specific characteristics:

- Humility
- Inspiring, motivating, encouraging
- Consistency
- Honesty
- Respect and care; value others
- Willingness to give honest feedback in a kind, gentle way
- Concern for others; looking out for the best interest of their employee(s) or mentee(s)

Helping others is something Millennials have been doing from an early age. They started working on community-service projects in high school or earlier. They find it gratifying to know they are helping others, which has helped them mature and develop character. Elizabeth stated that "my favorite part of it is that [younger Millennials] learn rather than dealing with their insecurities in a negative way; just go help someone else without thinking about yourself for a minute." It has also been a way to build leadership skills as they set goals, have a vision, and inspire others to support their efforts.

When asked who they admired, many of the Millennial leaders mentioned Blake Mycoskie, founder of TOMS® Shoes and a member of the Generation X cohort, because he demonstrates the entrepreneurial spirit that many Millennial leaders admire while serving as the ultimate role model of social responsibility.[1] The motivation behind starting the company was that he recognized a way to help people with a need. He saw children in Argentina who did not have shoes and created a company with a vision and business policy of donating one pair of shoes for these children for each pair of shoes sold. As Blake described it in an interview with Katherine Schwarzenegger, "Making money's fun, but making people have tears of joy? That's what life's all about."[2] Seeing the response from the grateful children inspires him. TOMS Shoes has now donated more than 60 million pairs of shoes to people in need. The company is now branching out into other areas, such as glasses for people who need them, coffee-bean growth to provide safe drinking water, and apparel to promote safe birth for babies and mothers in need.

When asked specifically about Millennial leaders they admired, many felt Millennials were still young and were not certain they had time to establish their influence yet. Several commended Jenna Bush Hager, Chelsea Clinton Mezvinsky, Meghan McCain, and Lauren Bush Lauren for their humanitarian efforts. Others in the entertainment industry were mentioned, but with some question as to their leadership or whether it was leadership in the right direction.

Social consciousness seems to be on the rise currently, and it does appear that awareness of social issues and commitment to volunteerism is more characteristic of some generations than others. The Traditionalist generation grew up in a time when everyone had to look out for each other during and following war and depression. Social consciousness was part of their daily life. Baby Boomers were much better cared for and counted their volunteer hours, spending a lot of time dedicated to the issues that were important to them. Finding time to fit volunteer hours into their workaholic lifestyle became more and more difficult for the younger Baby Boomers, as they were expected to produce more at work. Generation X had even less time for concern about social issues and volunteer efforts, as they had to follow the Baby Boomers in the workforce.

Well-Known Millennial Leaders Mentioned in Interviews

N MENTIONS	NAME & BIRTHYEAR	ACHIEVEMENTS, COMMENTS, REASONS FOR MENTION
9	Mark Zuckerberg (1984)	Cofounder, chairman, and CEO of Facebook; has passion and vision; probably not a good leader and not respected; referred to as "the guy who runs Facebook that everybody hates"
2	Jenna Bush Hager (1981)	Author and NBC *Today Show* news correspondent; projects to benefit AIDS and other charities; appears humble
2	Jessica Simpson (1980)	Recording artist, entertainer, and fashion designer; not a good example of a leader
1	Beyoncé (1981)	Singer, songwriter, actress; not a good example of a leader
1	Britney Spears (1981)	Recording artist and entertainer; probably not a leader in the right way
1	Chelsea Clinton (1980)	Works with the Clinton Foundation, Clinton Global Initiative, and is a special correspondent for NBC news; a good role model
1	Ivanka Trump (1981)	Executive VP of business development and acquisitions of the Trump Organization; also has a clothing and jewelry line; an influential leader who appears to keep work-life balance; advisor to President Donald Trump
1	Justin Bieber (1994)	Songwriter and musician; antibullying campaign; promoting Christianity
1	Kevin Systrom (1983)	Instagram cofounder; passion and motivation
1	Meghan McCain (1984)	Contributor to the *Daily Beast* and MSNBC; has written several books; a role model
1	Taylor Swift (1989)	Singer, songwriter; caring about others by helping flood victims
1	Lauren Bush Lauren (1984)	Cofounder, CEO, and creative director of FEED Projects, a nonprofit to fight world hunger; fashion designer; model; advocate for hungry children worldwide

Can you foster social consciousness?

Organizational leaders need to recognize that Millennials are interested in social consciousness, volunteering, community service, and the role their company has in local and global community efforts. If the company does not have a stated service program they are supporting, then the company's leadership team should think about developing one if they want to attract Millennials. If this is not an overall organizational goal, then another approach is to allow employees to establish efforts at an office, location, or project-team level to select a cause as their joint volunteer effort. At a minimum, the company can allow employees time off to pursue their own volunteer efforts during work hours. In this case, managers may need to recognize and accept that these employees will be taking time from work for volunteer activities. Providing a centralized reporting system or a newsletter with opportunities for recognition for their volunteer hours gives these employees a sense of accomplishment and a feeling that the company supports their efforts. This is also a good practice for recruitment.

Millennials who see there is little or no community service in a company are likely to decide the company is not a good fit for them. However, if they have overlooked the lack of volunteer opportunities through the company, and find themselves working with an organization they feel needs a social-consciousness program, they may propose a few good causes. After joining a team, if Millennials feel there is no support for the community or volunteer work they find rewarding and engaging, they are likely to feel the company does not fit their values and will soon be looking for another place to work.

The importance for Millennial leaders to feel they are working for an organization exhibiting social consciousness is being felt in the workplace currently as companies realize this is the reason they are losing Millennial workers to other companies with more social responsibility, to nonprofits, or to their own entrepreneurial ventures where they feel they can be more in line with their own values.

Takeaways

Millennials want to work for a company that has the same social-consciousness values they have. If these do not match, they will not stay at the company, so it is better to recognize this during the interview process. You may think this desire to do good is something that will go away once they get involved with the work, but that is not the case. Service is a way of life for them.

Millennial leaders also look to their leaders as examples of good social consciousness. When they don't see this, they question the similarity of their values. The leaders should at least be supportive of the efforts the Millennials are passionate about and allow them time to spend on volunteerism.

Leaders in today's organizations must recognize this community-service and social-awareness drive in their Millennial leaders if they want to keep them engaged and inspired in the vision of the company. Millennials expect to be able to spend time volunteering in activities that help others. Millennials are often misunderstood regarding their passion for giving back. What may be viewed by many older generations as a request for time off simply to get out of the office for volunteer work or free time is really a passion for community service. If the company leaders view this as a distraction from work and try to minimize their efforts, it can lead to conflict. Approaching their interest in volunteerism as a way to benefit the company through better employee engagement, community outreach, and marketing through increased brand awareness will lead to much happier employees and better results.

* * * * *

Helping others is natural in the view of Millennial leaders. Most have been involved in community-service activities since they were adolescents, and have always looked at helping others as a way to be socially conscious and to do the right thing.

Chapter 5

Leaders Do the Right Thing

A Leader Shows Others How

One Millennial leader described a woman he worked with who was very good at leading up in the organization. He recognized this was a unique skill and started going to her for advice. He wanted to learn this leadership skill that was beyond his own capabilities and that of most of the other leaders he worked with by observing her as an example. He was grateful for the time she would take to share her leadership skills with him. She did a presentation on giving and receiving feedback, and he was impressed that she took the initiative to give this presentation at an office lunch and learn. People came. She put herself on the line since it was outside her normal work responsibilities. She helped influence a lot of future leaders through this presentation and by taking time to help others. She led this Millennial leader to his own exploration of how to give and receive feedback and how to apply this to his own work. She wanted to help future leaders in the organization because she felt it was the right thing to do.

Ultimately, most of us want to do the right thing. Sometimes the choice is hard, but for Millennial leaders it doesn't seem that difficult. I repeatedly heard them say in a variety of ways that leaders *do the right thing,* often adding *for the right reasons.* It seemed so straightforward to them. Maybe they haven't had to face as many hard decisions, as much gray area, as many opportunities to bend the rules as leaders who are older. But I don't think that's the reason. It seems this age group understands "right" from "wrong" and wants to pick "right" for the right reasons.

As one leader expressed it to me, you often need to choose "that hard right over the easy wrong." That's part of being a leader, knowing in the long run it's for the best.

Study participants were almost absolute in their comments about leaders doing the right thing, enhanced by statements that leaders from previous generations had sometimes not done the right things, or had done what they thought was right at the time, but that it later became evident that some actions of leaders from previous generations were for the wrong reasons. Some reasons mentioned for leaders doing the right thing were:

- The leader had the right values.
- The leader was setting an example or showing others how.
- Previous generations did not do the right thing, and the results were bad.

How does a leader know what's right?

Examples of how participants described their understanding of doing the right thing can be found in their comments from their interviews. As Brandon described it, "[Leaders] genuinely just want to do the right thing. They really do. It's not 'Is it the right thing for me?' or the right thing for that or this. No, it's just genuinely the right thing. All things being cool, it's just the right thing to do. I think that's a solid trait you have to have at your core to be an ideal and a good leader."

Ashley considered the importance of doing the right thing as the leader setting an example to followers in her comment, "If I'm going to look to them as a leader, I'm going to be doing similar things to what my leader would be doing. If that's not right, then they shouldn't be doing it." Sarah was also concerned about the leader influencing followers in the right direction when she said, "That's really important in a leader, to make sure that their heart is in the right place if they are the one leading everyone to a common goal, and you want to know that the goal is worth achieving and not corrupt."

 "[Leaders] genuinely just want to do the right thing. They really do. It's not 'Is it the right thing for me?'"

Millennial leaders recognize it isn't always easy to do the right thing, but a leader needs to be able to make those choices. As Danielle described it, "Every day we make decisions to do what's right because it's the right thing to do, instead of choosing to take the easy alternative." Jessica believes, as a leader, she has to be able to make the right choices. "I think a good leader can stand alone and say 'I believe this. This might be harder or the less obvious route, but I've got to try it.'" Joshua recognizes the choices won't always be popular with everyone. "[As a leader], you have to make hard decisions that are going to affect people. Half the people will like it and half won't. You have to have the courage to make the right decisions based on your beliefs." Sarah recognizes there are people in the past who have faced these decisions. "There are CEOs that have retired that I identify with and respect and admire a lot that really did things the right way."

Are you doing the right thing in your work life?

Millennials are observing examples of "doing the right thing" in the leadership of the companies where they work, in their mentors, and in the other people they have contact with through work, regardless of their generation. Keeping Millennials engaged and developing a relationship of trust means making sure these Millennials see their company leadership does the right things for the well-being of others and the organization. This involves what is expected of leaders, such as truth, honesty, transparency, and concern for others.

Deciding the right thing to do is a reflection of the values, beliefs, preferences, and attitudes of each generational group. Millennials are more concerned with helping others and working with their peers than previous generations. This may create some differences in views about the right thing to do in a situation. The generation before them, Generation X, has been skeptical of organizations and their leadership, which has affected their interaction with others in the workforce. Baby Boomers gained a reputation for creating a competitive work environment, which may have generated an atmosphere that, in retrospect, led to some decision making that was not always for the right reasons. Today many companies have instituted a code of ethics that all employees must sign so they understand the expectations of ethical behavior and doing the right thing.

"You have to have the courage to make the right decisions based on your beliefs."

The values of the organization are reflected in the behavior of the managers. Many managers try not to let others see the core of their behavior, which reflects their true beliefs, preferences, and attitudes. This lack of transparency prevents the building of trust and an organizational culture based on shared values.

The Millennial generation doesn't hesitate to ask questions and expects to get answers. When decisions are made that impact employees and customers, Millennials expect their company and their leadership to do the right thing, whatever that may mean at the time. Not doing the right thing will give Millennials the impression that something is not right and that this is probably not a situation they want to be part of or leadership they want to follow.

Takeaways

Working with Millennials requires being aware of the outcome of the actions you take as a manager and the message it gives this highly transparent, socially conscious, and networked generation. They are tuned in to the actions taken toward employees and customers. Any hint that there was activity that was not the right thing to do or not done for the right reasons is not easily dismissed and would be questioned, and word spreads quickly through social media.

The right thing for the organization, for the leader in the organization, and for the Millennial leader may not be the same. When there are conflicting values or different views on right outcomes, this may be an indication of a bigger problem that needs to be resolved first. Keeping the Millennials' perspective in mind can be helpful when deciding the right thing to do. Depending on the situation, it may even be a good idea to ask a Millennial for input.

* * * * *

Millennial leaders share information about good work quickly through social media, and share their ideas about injustice and what they can do to correct the wrongs they see. They work together quickly through collaboration. They have always been a group that has been able to share thoughts and brainstorm ideas that are better by working together.

Chapter 6

Collaboration

Office Meetings

A Baby Boomer at a consulting firm told me his company had difficulty understanding what the Millennials were doing at work. A group of them would often go into a conference room and stay there for hours. It didn't appear to be a scheduled meeting with a start time, end time, or an agenda. He said, "We aren't sure what they are doing. In some ways, it seems like a party. They come up with some amazing ideas. The rest of us can't figure out how they do it."

Millennial leaders described their preferences in leaders and leadership as involving collaboration and sharing of knowledge. Participants discussed the importance of using networking and social media as part of collaborative work efforts when needed to research information or request immediate feedback.

In the interviews, the Millennial leaders described themselves as collaborative and demonstrated that they are relational. Their idea of a leader is an individual who is passionate and inspires others while working collectively with the team to accomplish the established goals. The participants confirmed the literature that shows Millennials prefer access to all levels in an organization, emphasizing their dislike for a hierarchical reporting structure, which they feel inhibits flexibility and information flow.[1] Millennial leaders don't like authoritarian leadership, illustrated by the continuing theme in the interviews of not wanting to be micromanaged. The leadership style of Millennials relies on sharing information and optimizing the use of technology, including social media. Many of these leaders are already moving into positions of power and influence.[2] The style used by Millennial leaders as they are learning to be leaders includes collaboration, relationship building, adaptability, and servant leadership.[3] Over time it will be interesting to see if Millennials' leadership style changes once they have more experience.

The socialization of Millennials reflected parental nurturing, protection, and praise far greater than any previous generation.[4] As children they were taught to work in groups, and school projects were usually team projects. They were the generation known for everyone being given a prize for participation, and winning wasn't the objective. As a result, Millennial cohort members exhibit confidence and optimism, combined with demands for immediate feedback and nearly continual recognition.[5] They value the close relationships they have built with their parents, other family members, and friends, and stay in constant contact with them.[6]

Generational Views of Collaboration and Team Orientation

Generation	View of Collaboration and Team Orientation
Traditionalists (1925–1945)	Top down; team leader makes the decisions
Baby Boomers (1946–1964)	Teamwork; work together to reach agreement and accomplish goals
Generation X (1965–1979)	Reach consensus; prefer not to meet in person
Millennials (1980–2000)	Collaborate; work together for the greater good

How do Millennials describe collaborative leadership?

To many of the Millennial leaders, collaboration is an essential part of their leadership style. As Sarah described it, "I try to get [team members] more involved. I try to include them in the process instead of doing everything myself and saying, 'This is how it's going to be.'" Nicole also looked at leadership more collaboratively when she said, "I think if I am able to inspire people to come along with me, it's more of a *with* than a *follow*. I hope to never become a leader that people follow; that's just dangerous. But how I interact with people that hopefully see me as a leader, I would say it is a lot about communication." Rachel's method of collaborating was also through connecting and communication. "I try to find ways to get connected with [peers] and interject different types of technology in their [areas], sort of getting them thinking about what they can do on their own."

Joshua described Millennial leaders as "adaptable, flexible, collaborative. Going along with collaborative is social networking." Ashley said that collaboration involved "encouraging [team members], and to see where they fit into the puzzle that is already there, and seeing what we can do better to let it be more cohesive, and how we could all work together to play a better game."

As part of collaboration, Millennial leaders discussed the importance of including others' ideas, especially their peers. They expect to be invited to contribute their ideas and feel discounted when they are not given an opportunity to state their views. Additionally, many Millennials addressed the importance of social media as tools for collaboration and how the advancements in technology have changed the way their generation communicates:

- Networking within and outside the organization for additional ideas
- Use of e-mail, blogging, Facebook, Twitter, YouTube, and new apps constantly becoming available
- The need to be adaptable and allow for role changes during collaboration

Collaboration is a characteristic of Millennial leaders and their generational cohort, in part, because of the availability of technology during their lifetimes. As leaders, Millennials rely on the skills they have learned for information gathering, which includes getting the views of their peers, their mentors, and more experienced leaders. The Millennial leaders interviewed were more accustomed to consolidating facts and ideas that emerged from a group than creating an individual work effort.

"I think if I am able to inspire people to come along with me, it's more of a *with* than a *follow*."

How can you benefit from Millennials' collaborative work style?

The introduction of Millennials as the most recent and potentially the largest generation to enter the workforce is having a significant impact on organizations, primarily because of their different perspective on values, beliefs, preferences, and attitudes about how and where they work. Allowing Millennials to work collaboratively on projects is essential to their productivity and ability to contribute to growth of the organization. They thrive on the ability to share ideas and create better, more innovative ideas by building on the thoughts of their peers. If the organization's leaders view this as being unable to think independently or time spent socializing or playing games, they will miss out on the opportunity to benefit from what this generation does best.

Millennial leaders are collaborative and use both their relational and technology skills to network. Leaders in the organizations where these Millennials are working will find they get better results and have happier Millennial leaders when they recognize how to incorporate this idea of collaboration into their work environment. While it may not work for their older employees, allowing Millennials to use social media for idea generation and giving them the opportunity to work in teams will empower them to embrace the goals of the organization and work hard to accomplish the objectives.

It may be difficult to accept a longer decision-making process as Millennials use their information gathering and collaborative style rather than the expected autonomous, more immediate decision capabilities Baby Boomers are accustomed to seeing in the workplace. It may appear that Millennials can't make a decision alone or reach a decision quickly. The other side of this is the value of a more informed decision that will have better buy-in from the people impacted because it considers the people who are affected by the decision.

Takeaways

As the Millennial leaders take on more leadership roles, the autocratic Traditionalists are moving out of the workforce and their type of leadership is also being replaced. The democratic Baby Boomers are starting to retire, but still have a significant influence on this next generation of leaders as they develop. The challenging, information-based, collaborative Generation X will be working together with Millennials and competing for many of the same positions. Although both of these younger generations are collaborative and comfortable with technology, Millennials are using networking and social media for information gathering and collaboration to give them an advantage as leaders.

* * * * *

Millennials have a global perspective as a result of their ability to travel and use the Internet; they are technologically literate and good at multitasking. This generation has had more exposure to technology than any previous generation, giving them a different outlook on the use of technology in their daily lives.

Chapter 7

Technology

Multitasking Millennial Mom

A Millennial leader, who is also a new mom just returning to work from maternity leave, sits at her desk at work with the door closed. She is on a conference call discussing plans for a meeting next month with other leaders in the company. While attending to the discussion, she is also looking at a social media site to investigate a potential problem she noticed with her baby, but isn't sure it warrants a visit to the pediatrician. Deciding everything is fine, she packs a small bag to visit her baby during her lunch hour, having just checked the webcam at daycare and seeing her young son peacefully taking his morning nap. She quickly checks another website for her volunteer activity to be sure the latest announcements had been posted regarding the upcoming fundraiser . . . all before finishing the conference call.

The Millennial generation has lived with technology from an early age, having grown up in a global world of multitasking, text messaging, and social media. The Millennial cohort is a group with worldwide impact because of the availability of technology and communications, and more freedom and access to move across borders and travel than prior generations. They are ambitious, having grown up in a child-centered environment, at home in a world dominated by technology and instant gratification, influenced by their Baby Boomer parents.

Millennials are technologically literate and good at multitasking. This generation has had more exposure to technology than any previous generation, with access to personal computers and cell phones since early childhood. This ability to use technology as a tool and familiarity with it to quickly access information often gives Millennials an advantage in the workplace over coworkers of other generational groups. The Internet has also provided Millennials with the ability to travel virtually.

 "Millennials are technologically literate and good at multitasking."

It was evident from the interviews that Millennial leaders believed they were different from previous generations, and their use of technology and social media to access information and their peers made them unique in their ability to be more collaborative and inclusive than any prior generation.

How do Millennials use technology and social media?

Rachel was surprised to learn what an advantage her understanding of technology became for her in her work. Rachel's view of leadership was based on examples and showing others how to lead. She first realized she was a leader when she won a leadership award, and she then used her leadership skills to help others understand and adopt technology. Rachel commented, "I try to find ways to get connected with [peers] and interject different types of technology in their [areas], sort of getting them thinking about what they can do on their own."

Melissa surmised, "A leader should be direct and very clear about his or her expectations, yet kind and open minded, accepting that Millennials use technology and have different ways of doing things than other generations."

Additionally, many participants addressed the importance of social media as tools for collaboration and how technology has changed the way their generation communicates. As the most collaborative generation in the workplace, each new social media app or technology tool becomes an opportunity for them to work together more efficiently. Since Millennials like to work in teams and are goal oriented and skilled in the use of technology, they are willing to test new technology and adopt the tools they find easy to use and beneficial to them both as individuals and groups. Most Millennial leaders are more casual in their attitudes and approaches to work, more collaborative and inclusive, and rely more on technology, including social media, for access to information and networking with peers than coworkers from other generational groups.

Millennials have always had technology in their lives; therefore, it is natural to them to use a variety of different technology methods, including social media and the Internet, as part of their ability to collaborate and work with their peers. Millennial leaders understand how to use their comfort level with technology to their advantage for better communications, quicker access to information, better presentation of materials, and in many other ways to accomplish their work with impressive outcomes.

How can different views of technology impact organizations?

Millennials want to work in teams and are goal oriented, confident, and service oriented,[1] which may not be what their bosses expect. They are ambitious and skilled in the use of technology.[2] They are willing to work hard, expecting immediate gratification and quick advancement in return.[3] This is not always the work environment they enter when they finally find a job where they will be working with Generation Xers, Baby Boomers, and possibly some Traditionalists who are still in the workforce.

The challenging, information-based, collaborative Generation Xers will be working together with Millennials and competing for many of the same positions. Although both groups are comfortable with technology, Millennials are using networking and social media for information gathering and collaboration with their peers to give them an advantage as leaders.

 "A leader should be direct and very clear about his or her expectations, yet kind and open minded, accepting that Millennials use technology and have different ways of doing things than other generations."

The leadership style of Millennials relies on sharing information and optimizing the use of technology, including social media. Often managers of Millennial leaders view their use of technology as a waste of time, assuming it is time spent playing games, chatting with friends through social media, or searching for the latest entertainment news. However, this time is also likely to be spent searching for data, alternate views, trends, the latest news, and information that can be used to enhance their assignment.

Millennial leaders prefer to share responsibility, using a participative style of leadership and relying on their ability to network and their experience with technology, such as social media, to enhance this capability.

In addition to being technology oriented and skilled at multitasking, Millennials are known for their short attention spans.[4] One aspect of Millennials' lack of leadership training may be the lack of training presented in a format that interests them or is suited to their learning styles and/or ability to learn. Providing them with information in a format that will maintain their interest will help keep them involved and educated.

The Millennials' combined ability to multitask and use technology for quick problem solving is often one of the sources of generational conflict. This has given them the ability to focus on an issue or assignment, get it done, and move on. For older generations, especially Baby Boomers, it can be hard to understand how quality work can be done so quickly. And in reverse, Millennials view Baby Boomers as hard working but lacking in productivity because their methods of accomplishing the same tasks often take longer.

Takeaways

Millennials use technology to solve problems. They are likely to jump to Google or one of many social media sites when asked to find something. When they start searching on their electronic devices, it doesn't mean you have lost them from the conversation. They are probably multitasking, trying to help you find the answer to whatever you have just asked. Millennials are also likely to be satisfied to find an answer and consider the problem solved unless they are asked to do more research. With so much information at their fingertips, it is easy to get lost or distracted when researching online. If you ask a Millennial a question, you will probably get an answer and no additional information. If you want additional information, you need to explain what else you want.

Millennials are not your IT department. They are comfortable with using technology, which means they are familiar with many applications and have technology at their fingertips for problem solving. That does not mean they know how it works or can help you with your applications, which may be completely different. They may be able to and may be patient enough to help you, but they aren't the generation that invented this technology, and many of them aren't that interested in how it works; they are just skilled at using it. Those skills also do not translate to fixing the projector or the TV remote. They may be able to help with that, but they don't like the assumption that because they are Millennials, they can do anything with technology. It can be embarrassing when they can't, because a lot of it doesn't make sense to them either. They may be completely bored with the outdated technology being used.

* * * * *

The Millennials' familiarity with technology often gives them an advantage over older workers who may take longer to learn new technology as it is introduced into the workplace. These situations can create workplace conflict due to resentment by employees from older generations. Mentoring provides an opportunity for different generations to learn from each other.

Chapter 8

Mentoring

Girl Talk

When Haley Kilpatrick was in middle school, she thought she was the only one who suffered through those difficult times girls go through. She found valuable advice from a few older mentors, especially a high school girl she met through her school dance team. After Haley made it through those tough years and noticed her younger sister was facing the same middle school difficulties, she realized she could take the valuable lessons she learned of having a high school girl mentor a middle school girl through this difficult time. She proposed a well-organized plan to start an organization to her principal, and a wonderfully successful program called Girl Talk was born. Girl Talk's basic premise consists of high school girls leading middle school girls in weekly discussion groups about everything from body-image issues, self-respect, dealing with mean girls, bullying, meeting guys, and getting along with their parents. The organization is free to members and emphasizes peer-to-peer mentoring and volunteering in the community. Having recently celebrated its ten-year anniversary, the organization has served more than sixty thousand middle and high school girls in forty-eight states and seven countries. (www.mygirltalk.org)

Millennial leaders interviewed described mentors as an important part of their development process and commented that they viewed mentors as individuals upon whom they relied for guidance. Many of them discussed the characteristics of an effective mentor, or how a certain mentor helped them. They also mentioned mentoring others, because they saw that it was important to continue their growth through learning to develop others.

These Millennial leaders stated that mentors were an important part of their development and growth in their leadership roles. They were grateful for the time these individuals gave them and expected their mentors to set examples and be role models. Participants considered investing in others through mentoring to be an important aspect of leadership.

The selfless nature of Millennial leaders (from their own perspectives as leaders and the perspective of their expectations of leaders) was evident from their comments in the interviews as they discussed helping others and their preference for leaders who give back by mentoring and advising others.

 These Millennial leaders stated that mentors were an important part of their development and growth in their leadership roles. They were grateful for the time these individuals gave them and expected their mentors to set examples and be role models. Participants considered investing in others through mentoring to be an important aspect of leadership.

What is the role of a mentor?

Heather described mentors as individuals she could reach out to for advice on how they would handle a situation, thinking of them at various times when facing conflict or crisis management. From her perspective, they understood "life is just life and we're all in this situation, and we just have to fix it and keep moving on." Heather would also ask her mentors questions such as "How did you overcome this barrier?" or "How did you make yourself more influential?" or "How did you take on this leadership role?" She talked to her mentors before taking on any new situation: "How did you manage your time, or how did you manage this situation?" Heather noticed that from the outside, it looked like everyone else but her had their lives under control. At those times she would go to her mentors and leaders to ask them, "How did you juggle this? When was the stopping point? How much time did you give yourself?"

Elizabeth felt that she owed a lot of her success to her "awesome mentors," and Sarah commented that her mentor "taught her a lot about leadership." Jessica appreciated having great mentors to go to who could "weigh both sides of a problem."

Amber made a point to find mentorship because she realized that most people have common problems and learn by sharing their experiences. As Amber described it, "I found great value in having my mentors tell me how they handled a situation or viewed a problem, even if it wasn't exactly the same as what I was dealing with, because I could find the common issues and figure out how to apply this to my situation or use it later with a different problem."

Elizabeth stated, "You need leaders who are more advanced than you and not just totally idealistic for mentors."

Ashley said, "Recently I was considering applying for another job, and I talked to my mentors about it and ultimately decided that wasn't what I wanted to do . . . they were able to listen to where I saw myself going professionally and could also see what I'm doing now. They provided me some guidance, saying, 'Let's look at it this way—do you like what you are doing now? What have you mastered?' [They] helped me look at the big picture of making a strategic career move, and gave me some ideas on things I wouldn't have thought about before getting this type of guidance and leadership."

Mentoring is a key component of leadership development to Jessica, as she depends on her mentors for guidance and has a passion for mentoring young women. Jessica believes two important qualities of a leader are consistency and caring about others. According to Jessica, Millennial leaders often prefer to work with other Millennials because they are technologically savvy, but she felt many of them do not recognize that they lack the wisdom that comes with experience, so she received insight from her mentors.

Participants felt that leaders should be examples to their followers and demonstrate leadership through their actions. Investing in others through mentoring was considered an important aspect of leadership to the participants.

Millennial leaders recognized that they needed to learn more about leadership in order to be the great leaders they strive to be. Their preferred methods of learning leadership skills are continuous learning through mentoring and training that includes hands-on experiences with guidance from experienced leaders, including their mentors. Many of these leaders felt their method of learning had been from negative experiences, which may not have been the best way to learn. As they learn to be good leaders, they are anxious to share what they learn by mentoring younger leaders.

"You need leaders who are more advanced than you and not just totally idealistic for mentors."

Do you have a mentorship program?

Organizations will change as they recognize the need for mentoring programs for their future leaders. Training programs to meet the requirements for Millennial leaders' development need to be established within the organization or funded as external programs. The shifting view of a leader, from the Traditionalist's perspective as the top of the hierarchy holding the position that was earned by time on the job, to the Baby Boomer view of the position that was earned by consensus as the best person for the job, to the Generation X view that the leader was the most competent person, is now replaced by the Millennials' expectation that the leader is the best person to guide others.

The information obtained through my research benefits Millennial leaders as they seek mentoring and guidance to assist them in their growth toward becoming future leaders, providing a better understanding of Millennial leaders' beliefs, values, preferences, and expectations in leadership roles. Research results assist in determining the types of coaching, training, mentoring, and leadership development needed by Millennial leaders.

Organizations that are interested in hiring and keeping Millennial leaders will benefit from investing in mentoring programs. The rewards can be in many areas:

- Millennials will feel they are part of the company and get involved much faster, overcoming the feeling of not being heard.
- Millennials will understand the corporate culture and become committed sooner to the values and goals.
- Leaders who become mentors will relate to the Millennials and understand their view because they know them better by working directly with them.

Their familiarity with technology often gives Millennial leaders an advantage over older workers who may take longer to learn new technology as it is introduced into the workplace. These situations can create workplace conflict due to resentment by employees from older generations, or such situations can become building blocks for better relationships as opportunities for collaboration or reverse mentoring.

Another option for mentoring can be group mentoring programs, which are less demanding on senior managers but can still be an effective way to give Millennial leaders the feedback they desire. Coaching can be accomplished through face-to-face meetings, conference calls, webcasts, and online discussions.[1] New hires learn the ropes faster and training costs are reduced. Many Millennials like the added benefit of seeing what types of issues their peers are having and how their shared mentor approaches different types of problems.

Takeaways

Millennials expect their leaders to invest in helping them through mentoring and guidance; however, they do not want to be micromanaged or told exactly what to do. This can create generational misunderstanding when an older mentor advises a Millennial on a situation and later discovers the advice was not followed. The Millennial mentee likely took that advice under consideration when making the decision and may use the advice in a later situation. The older mentor may have felt his or her time was wasted. However, it wasn't. The advice was likely considered and not forgotten; the Millennial considered it part of the leadership learning process along with the success or failure that resulted from the decision that was ultimately made.

Different generations often express their values in different ways, which can lead to conflict. As the workforce moves from traditional worker values of Traditionalists and Baby Boomers, to more emergent worker values held by Generation X and Millennials, a shift in values places an emphasis on nurturing and mentoring of younger employees.

* * * * *

Millennials look to mentors as role models and want to learn from their experiences. It is important to Millennial leaders that these mentors and other leaders they respect are responsible for their actions and can be counted on to do what they say they will do.

Chapter 9

Leaders Do What They Say

Coach

One Millennial leader described an incident that happened when he was a senior in high school. He said he had heard there was a party, including alcohol, and that a lot of his classmates went. The next week, his coach asked each player to go into his office and tell him if he had been at the party. Everyone knew the coach knew who had been there and who had been drinking underage, which was against baseball rules. The coach found out that some of the students at the party were some of the team's best players. Each player who had been at the party had to sit out the next game, even though the team was in the middle of divisional playoffs. The school and the parents wanted to win. The players realized they had been protected from consequences in the past, but the coach benching them was going to happen whether or not it was what they wanted. The team ended up doing well, but it was a difficult time. The coach had a bigger goal than the success of that one season—he wanted the students on the team to learn that choices have consequences, and that rules are rules. The Millennial leader who told me this story really respected the coach for sticking to his word, and never forgot the lesson he learned from that incident.

Millennial leaders frequently talked in their interviews about leaders actually doing what they say, not saying one thing and doing another. Several individuals discussed the importance of seeing leaders carry through on their commitments.

As individuals become leaders over time and through experience, they develop as leaders through observation of other leaders, including role models, feedback, and practice.[1] Good leaders learn to identify their own goals, values, and ambitions, becoming self-aware and capable of self-leadership.[2]

People often view the important leadership characteristic known as credibility differently. This is especially true when looking at the varying generational cohorts. Traditionalists are accustomed to leading by command and control. They have spent many years working in environments where the leaders at the top of the organizations gave orders and were not to be questioned. Baby Boomers are more questioning and look to their leaders as role models. They are the group that created the concept of teamwork in the organization, preferring consensus in decision making. Generation X questions positional authority and is much more concerned with the competency of their leaders. Millennial leaders seek transparency and expect to learn leadership skills from their leaders, whom they believe should serve as examples and mentors. It is important that the leaders they admire and follow do what they say they will do for these optimistic Millennials who feel they are ready to take on big challenges.

The Millennial leaders interviewed regarded the theme of leaders doing what they say as an important aspect of leadership for several reasons:

- Leaders need to keep their commitments to be respected.
- Leaders should be able and willing to do things they talk about doing.

- Leaders who are not showing followers how to make good choices are not good leaders.

Why is it important to Millennial leaders to keep commitments?

Millennial leaders respect leaders who keep commitments and view this as an important aspect of leadership. As Brandon stated, "I respond well to people who do what they say, do it for the right reasons, actually go make a difference, and don't just sit around with an opinion talking about it all the time. I respond very well to people like that because I respect them."

Millennials feel it is important for leaders to set examples. Ashley commented, "It's part of the whole *show them and don't tell them*. If my boss is not going to take something seriously, then why should I? If I'm going to look to them as a leader, I'm going to be doing similar things to what my leader would be doing. If that's not right, then they shouldn't be doing it."

Being a leader requires acting like a leader, which means being present and committed. Michael said, "The few comments I've gotten [from people I manage] sounded something like, 'My last manager always scheduled one-on-ones but never showed up. I'm really glad you show up.'" Jennifer had a different experience with a leader who failed to act like a leader. She described it as "his failure to manage expectations and include others in the conversations [that] made it difficult for us to consider him a leader. He was able to accomplish the goals but was not good at leading by example and teaching others what needed to be done. Overall, I didn't consider that good leadership."

When Melissa described how important she felt it was that she keep her commitments as a leader, she said, "If I acted a certain way, you know, not being the person I should be, or not making great choices, they were going to follow that, because that was what they saw. I feel like that responsibility and that role was really, really powerful."

"I respond well to people who do what they say, do it for the right reasons, actually go make a difference . . ."

Brandon also raised the idea of commitment when he talked about his view of an ideal leader: "I think another consistent trait among these individuals is the fact that they also do what they say. Very few people do what they say. Ideal leaders do what that say. Their actions speak infinitely louder than their words, because they say it and then they go do it. Then people realize they're doing it and it's working and they should do that, too. It's like trying to tell someone what being burned when you touch a hot stove is. You can't do it. You tell somebody all day long not to touch a hot stove because they'll get burned. They don't understand the concept of burned or hot and it's pointless. They are going to touch it and get burned, and it's a bad thing. So just speaking ideals, philosophies, and process doesn't mean anything if you can't do it and show what it actually means to them. So an ideal leader does what they say . . . A good leader leads by example."

Elizabeth commented that the leader understands the influence he or she has on others who are watching his or her actions. "I define leadership as a person who, whether it's at work or in extracurricular activities or in their community, thinks before they act, because they know that there are other people watching how they act and modeling their behaviors after them. A leader is . . . someone who hopefully is really thoughtful about what they say and do, because there are people reporting to them or looking up to them."

Heather described a great example of how important it can be to a Millennial leader to show that as a leader, they will do what they say they will do. After being elected treasurer of an organization, she said, "I stood up and yelled, 'I'll be the best damn treasurer you've ever seen!' I tried very hard and I did a good job. I spent the money very well and kept good records. People trusted me in that role. I guess that's part of being a leader. Doing what you say you are going to do."

Justin described a situation that was very disillusioning for him as a Millennial leader: "I worked at a company where we knew something was wrong and the leaders denied it. . . . The owners would say everything was fine and revenues were fine. This was after hundreds of layoffs, and everyone knew something was wrong. They continued to tell us everything was fine. That's just not good. That's not instilling confidence in the people they are leading. Once that happens, everything's falling apart."

Are you true to your word at work?

Millennial leaders look to their leaders as role models, and we've already seen how they expect leaders to be honest. If the leader can't or won't do what they say, they feel something isn't right. If there is a good reason, then an explanation is called for, but that probably should have been thought of before making a commitment. Here are some best approaches when leading Millennials:

- Only make commitments you can and will keep.
- If you can't keep a commitment for a good reason, such as plans changed, be honest about it.
- If you think you are too important to do something and the Millennial should be doing it, think again. They will sense this, and it could lead to resentment. You might enjoy working together. If you just can't bring yourself to that, then be honest.

From an organizational view, it is important to show Millennials they can trust the organization to be true to its word. Projects change and priorities change, but that isn't the same as a company that shows a lack of vision or direction and doesn't keep its commitments to the employees. Leaders within the organization or other leaders are expected to do what they say they will do. These are the individuals Millennials look to as examples and learn from. Millennial leaders also count on their peers to do what they say. They trust each other to be there, supporting them in their collaborative roles.

Regarding the importance Millennials place on trust, they expect to be able to trust a leader to keep commitments. They value transparency and can understand when there is an unexpected change, but lose trust when there is lack of communication.

Takeaways

Millennials are watching their leaders, mentors, and role models as their examples and continuously learning what to do based on what they see. When they see leaders who do not do what they say they will, it is discouraging and has to be sorted through as an example to learn from. It's not the way Millennials want to work, so it is likely they will see it as a bad learning experience, and the leader's credibility is significantly damaged by that action.

Millennials want to be able to trust their leaders and have confidence in them. Unfortunately, many of the Millennial leaders said they learned how to lead by watching others, and deciding which attributes of poor leaders they would not incorporate into their leadership style. Being let down by leaders who did not keep their word was one of the areas where Millennials wanted to be different from many of the leaders they observed.

If the organization does not do what it said it would, the Millennial will question the organization. If plans change, Millennials want to understand the reason for the change in direction, or at a minimum an acknowledgment that there was a change in direction. The sudden abandonment of the old plan and adoption of a new plan makes it appear that something is being hidden from them.

Leaders shirk commitments for a number of reasons, including forgetting their promises, not caring, or determining there are higher priorities. None of these show good leadership to the Millennial unless there is acknowledgment and transparency. If, as a leader, you committed to do something, it is better to get it done, if possible, since there must have been a good reason for making the commitment.

Millennial leaders are true to their word in working with their peers and their organization. Frequently, they will do whatever they committed to do immediately so it will not be hanging over their heads. They are more likely to not commit to something if they are not sure they can complete the task. They may even tell you they will look into it or research it, then come back with the task completed.

* * * * *

Working with leaders who do what they say is important to Millennial leaders because they expect to be able to count on others as they plan their work and personal activities. This gives them the ability to manage their time and their priorities so they can focus on having time for work, family, friends, and community service, helping them attain the work-life balance they are looking for.

Chapter 10

Work-Life Balance

What is work-life balance?

I asked a Millennial leader to describe the attributes of a leader who would best manage her.

This was her response:

[My ideal boss is] definitely one who values innovation and creativity, and tells you they value it. [A leader] who is very straightforward with you but tactful. I respond well to loving, kind, and compassionate leaders, and people who are not fake. I cannot stand when a boss is phony or you find out they have a history of lying. Basically, I want my leader to be perfect. Not lie. If you mess up, then tell me honestly in a really cool, constructive, creative way that you messed up so that we can both learn from it. I want [my leader] to have a work-life balance. A family. I get so frustrated when I have female leaders who aren't married and don't have kids; I think, *Well I don't actually want to be like you anymore. Because I want to have it all and you haven't succeeded at that.* So I'm really hard on leaders. I want them to take time to take care of themselves . . . to do yoga, get massages . . . that kind of stuff. I value that a lot.

Work-life balance was a topic the participants pointed out as being unique for their generation. Millennial leaders are passionate about their work, but they are also passionate about their friends, their families, and their volunteer activities. To Millennial leaders, work-life balance involves fitting all of these activities into their busy, multitasking lives.

Recent research has examined changes in the impact of generational-cohort shifts, as Traditionalists became a small percentage of the work population and Baby Boomers started to retire. New research on the changing view of work-life balance shows that Millennials put friends and family ahead of work.

A study of Millennial graduate students showed these leaders are redefining diversity, humility, and work-life balance as they enter the workforce and interact with older generations.[1] They value family and friends over work and have a perspective of work-life balance that is different from other generational cohorts. Research shows that Generation Xers and Millennials wanted to compress their development plans, yet did not want to let work stifle their work-life balance. Although money was typically more important than recognition to the Traditionalists and Baby Boomers, work-life balance and job satisfaction were usually more important than job promotion for the Generation Xers and Millennials.

How do Millennials define work-life balance?

Millennial leaders preferred leaders and role models who were balanced, which applied to work-life balance and the ability to manage multiple aspects of work. A balanced lifestyle was important to Millennial leader Amanda, so it was important for her to see leaders with work-life balance or life-work balance; determining the right order was significant to Millennials, according to Amanda, as she stressed the emphasis on life and living being a priority over work for Millennials. She shared her preference for a leader with a good heart and an interest in volunteer work, especially one who cared about work-life balance.

Elizabeth appreciated a role model leader who would "take that opportunity to teach me something, and empower me to not make that mistake again. If I did something well, she would tell me, but she wouldn't overdo it, like a lot of people do. She would make sure that my work-life balance was, in fact, balanced."

Millennial leaders stressed the importance of relationships with mentors, family members, and friends while expressing their desire to have a good work-life balance. Mentors and older family members provided insight and assistance with the experience the Millennial leaders deemed valuable to their ability to be a good leader. In discussions around work-life balance, these Millennial leaders showed an understanding that not everyone has the same view, and that Millennials have their own interpretation of work-life balance, recognizing that living in a technologically connected world allowed them to work anytime and anywhere yet still have time for their personal lives.

 Millennial leaders preferred leaders and role models who were balanced, which applied to work-life balance and the ability to manage multiple aspects of work.

Millennials value family and friends more than work, thus maintaining their close relationships with their parents, other family members, and friends, staying in constant contact with them. The importance of work-life balance to Millennials begins with this desire to have time for family and friends, and then extends to the desire to have time for volunteer activities and personal time. The continued desire to give back to their community drives Millennial leaders to devote personal time to community service and to prefer working for an organization that has a commitment to social responsibility.

How do you achieve work-life balance?

It is important to recognize that work-life balance has a new balance with Millennials, especially for the leaders who are concerned about making time for all of their activities. Work-life balance and job satisfaction are usually more important than job promotion for Millennials, who put family and friends first. Organizations need to recognize this desire for work-life balance and satisfy Millennials without upsetting older generations by making them feel there is favoritism. Millennials often value flexibility over money, which gives businesses the opportunity to offer rewards in terms of time off, flexible hours, or pay, thus appealing to each generation in their desired manner.

The different views of work and work-life balance create generational conflict in the workplace. The lack of understanding of priorities and how each group perceives work and accomplishes work generates distrust among the various groups. Looking at their various work ethics and understanding of work-life balance provides insight into these misunderstandings. The Traditionalist generation was accustomed to keeping work and family life separate. The workaholic Baby Boomers believed that time in the office showed dedication to the job, and work-life balance was a juggling act. Generation X used their creativity and desire for change to look for work-life balance and became the group who introduced the concept of telecommuting. When Millennials work on the go using their mobile devices to incorporate work, family, friends, and community service into a continuous stream during the day, older generations often see them as irresponsible or goofing off without even taking time to recognize the accomplishments of this multitasking generation.

Changes in Work-Life Balance

Generation	How They View Work	What's Work-Life Balance?
Traditionalists	Sacrifice, hard work, respect for authority, separation of work and family	Balance involves defined roles keeping work and home life separated.
Baby Boomers	Long hours, teamwork, consensus	Balance means juggling everything while I look for meaning in my life.
Generation X	Self-reliance, creativity, adaptability	I want to find balance now, not when I'm sixty-five years old.
Millennials	Speed, networking, problem solving, engaging with authority, meeting challenges with optimism	Work isn't everything. I need flexibility so I can balance all my activities (family, friends, and community service).

Takeaways

As organizations prepare for the advancement of more leaders from the Millennial generational cohort, the current leaders can expect to see more demands for work-life balance; flatter, more participative teams; and leaders who challenge higher levels in the organization to consider their creative, innovative ideas.

* * * * *

Along with balancing family, friends, work, and volunteer activities, Millennial leaders still feel it is important to continue learning to be better leaders. As part of their busy, multitasking lives, they look to their mentors, their peers, their relationships with their family, and their volunteer work as opportunities for growth. They often choose to work on projects at work or in the community because they see these as learning experiences. Many Millennial leaders are returning to graduate school either part time or full time to enhance their educations.

Chapter 11

Continuous Learning

Lifelong Learning

When I asked Millennial leaders to describe a real-life learning experience they had as leaders, many of them told me they had learning experiences every day. They are always looking for ways to improve and be better leaders. One leader who works in social media said she had a blog called Lifelong Learning because she knew she would never stop learning and she respected that in other leaders. Like many of the Millennial leaders, she wanted to receive more constructive criticism as a learning tool.

Millennial leaders interviewed felt they were still learning to be leaders. Some stated that this was because they were young and leadership was new to them; others felt that being a good leader always involved learning and evolving. After all, this generation is known for being the most educated group of young adults to ever enter the workforce. In spite of this, many older workers seem amazed by how much these young workers don't know. There seems to be a lack of practical knowledge and a shift in the emphasis of what is being taught in school, leaving a very educated group of people with a lack of certain knowledge and skills.

Continuous learning, as part of being a good leader, requires constantly learning new skills and adapting to situations:

- Learning to be a leader requires experience.
- Mentors are valuable in assisting with learning leadership.
- Being a good leader is an evolutionary process.
- Learning involves continuous improvement.

How do Millennials view learning opportunities?

Like previous generations who entered the workforce regardless of the era, Millennials don't know what they don't know. Just recognizing that you have a lot to learn is a great starting point. As Elizabeth aptly stated, "I think I have a long way to go. I wish I could say there's someone in my generation that didn't have a long way to go, but we're young." However, she also commented, "I think we're not going to get there if the forty- and fifty-year-olds keep pushing us down and ignoring us and getting frustrated, and saying we're not what they know, so we're not okay, so they're not going to invest in us. I think it sucks to have our future and our world be affected by them, and I wish that we could just skip them," which illustrates the frustration with the older generations in the workforce who appear to be roadblocks.

Millennial leaders understand they are still growing into their roles as leaders. As Justin said, "I think in order to be a leader you have to have a lot of experience, and you have to endure any setbacks, any shortfalls." He also had a strong belief that you learn from everyone, so you should listen attentively to everything, which is more characteristic of Millennials than any of the older generations, who are more likely to be selective about to whom they will pay attention.

Rachel expressed another side of learning by experience when she said, "I think my leadership development has been experiential. I have had to learn as I go." Many Millennial leaders have expressed that, even though they may have taken leadership training or other types of courses to prepare them for leadership or the work environment, the most valuable things they have learned were not taught by someone else, but rather learned through an experience.

Learning involves others, including elders, mentors, and peers. Heather felt there were a lot of leaders her age, but in terms of truly understanding how to be a leader, she turned to mentors who were much older, while still keeping a network of people her age. She met with both networks regularly and asked questions like, "What are you doing to stay active in the community? What are you doing to network? How do you stay connected?"

From her experience with a great leader, Nicole learned that effective mentoring is an ongoing process that happens gradually. As she stated, "You learn the [company] from the ground up when you are doing that. . . . You are [doing the work]. And some days you don't feel terribly excited about that. But I'll never forget what I learned. She was teaching me. And you don't know it at the time. When you are with a good leader, it's not [until] much later that you realize they are leading you."

Learning from experience is an evolutionary process. As Heather says, "I always look for ways to improve. You can always be a better leader." Recognizing that it takes practice to get better at the process is important. As Rachel described her approach, she said, "I think you have to be able to step back and really look at yourself, if you are a leader, and reflect and say, 'This really did not go well,' and see yourself objectively, and always try to do better." Or as Sarah so succinctly described her learning experiences, "So that was a crash-and-burn learning experience," and then she moved on.

Michael described his view: "The idea of using experience as growth, I think, is actually something that people younger than me sort of exhibit and agree with more than I think people exactly my age. You know it's weird, being thirty-one years old; I'm right on the cusp. Sometimes I see things in people older than me I really relate to. This aspect I'm describing now (using experience as growth), I really relate to people younger than me."

 Many Millennial leaders have expressed that, even though they may have taken leadership training or other types of courses to prepare them for leadership or the work environment, the most valuable things they have learned were not taught by someone else, but rather learned through an experience.

Most Millennials recognize that they need constructive criticism. As Amanda said, "I honestly wish that I got more constructive criticism, because that's going to help me. I know I'll never stop learning, so I respect that in other leaders." Michael liked learning by having continuously changing roles in his job. As he described it, "Each day you had a different role. Every single day I was learning something new, in what I felt were pretty stressful situations."

The Millennial leader participants recognized that they were inexperienced and still growing and developing as leaders. For that reason, continuous learning became a theme throughout the interviews. Many of the participants stated their desire to learn to be a better leader or their hope to have the opportunity for leadership training. Many relied on their mentors to help them.

How does training take place?

The research for this book also illustrates that Millennial leaders recognize that they need to learn more about leadership in order to be the great leaders they strive to be. Their preferred methods of acquiring leadership skills are continuous learning through mentoring and training that includes hands-on experiences with guidance from experienced leaders. Many of these leaders felt their method of learning had been from negative experiences, which can be discouraging. As they begin to understand how to be good leaders, they are anxious to share what they learn by mentoring younger leaders.

Their training had a variety of formats, such as a leadership program in college or graduate school, leadership training through their company or an association, or leadership development through mentoring. However, their training had not provided them with enough examples of how to be leaders. Instead, they had learned through experience, and more of it was negative experience as they witnessed examples of poor leadership. The participants felt they needed more training to be good leaders, but did not have specific training planned.

Millennials desire and seek out training rather than waiting for someone to arrange it for them. Effective training in the organizations where Millennials want to work will offer a variety of options, taking advantage of multimedia and the flexibility to take the training whenever and wherever it is convenient. It is frequently assumed that because of their high use of technology, Millennials want all of their training to be computer based. The ability to learn what would be needed to perform the job well seemed most important to Millennials, recognizing that this may take on various forms such as multimedia, classroom, computer-based, and on-the-job training.

Training also takes place daily through mentoring and leading by example. Millennials view each experience as a training opportunity. As their leader, it's important to remember to use work situations as coaching for Millennials. It's also important to remember they will be observing your behavior as part of their leadership training.

Takeaways

Millennials view training as a reward. Offering training as an incentive can be motivating for Millennials. Their view of rewards is different from other generations, who may see training as required or something you figure out for yourself, and may prefer time off, flex time, or financial rewards.

Millennials feel they must have training in order to be successful. They are anxious to do a good job and want the proper training. They are willing to ask for it, feeling this will help them advance in their careers.

Millennials feel the organization is investing in them by providing training. They are always looking for opportunities for growth and view coaching as a way to improve and grow. They also appreciate the investment the company is making in them by providing them with training.

Millennials like training in a variety of formats. They multitask well and are comfortable with various media. It is best to give them training in a variety of formats using the most effective format for the subject of the training, including on-the-job training.

* * * * *

Continuous training gives Millennials the ability to improve their skills and develop the leadership qualities they admire in others.

Conclusion

The research used for the basis of this book has demonstrated that Millennial leaders have their own unique leadership style. As an emerging group of leaders, they will be influential in organizations in the future. The leadership style of Millennials is more collaborative and inclusive than that of previous generations. Millennial leaders prefer to share responsibility, using a participative style of leadership and relying on their ability to network and their experience with technology, such as social media, to enhance this capability. Their strong moral values provide the foundation for their trust in others, the importance of honesty, their desire to do the right thing, and their reasons for caring about others. At the same time, they are innovative and creative in ways of looking at work and passionate about what they believe in and want to work on. Work-life balance has shifted with Millennials, putting family and friends first, especially for the leaders who are concerned about making time for all of their activities.

Millennial leaders recognize that they need to learn more about leadership in order to be the great leaders they strive to be. Their preferred methods of learning leadership skills are continuous learning through mentoring and training that includes hands-on experiences with guidance from experienced leaders. Many of these leaders felt their method of learning had been from negative experiences, which may not have been the best way to learn. As they learn to be good leaders, they are anxious to share what they learn by mentoring younger leaders.

As organizations prepare for the advancement of more leaders from the Millennial generational cohort, the current leaders can expect to see more demands for work-life balance; flatter, more participative teams; and leaders who challenge higher levels in the organization to consider their creative, innovative ideas. Millennial leaders will continue to prefer to work with companies where they feel valued, sense that there is honesty and trust, observe that leaders keep their commitments, and note that social responsibility is one of the goals.

As the Millennial leaders take on more leadership roles, the autocratic Traditionalists are moving out of the workforce, and their type of leadership is also being replaced. The democratic Baby Boomers are starting to retire, but still have a significant influence on this next generation of leaders as they develop as leaders. The challenging, information-based, collaborative Generation X will be working together with Millennials and competing for many of the same positions. Although both Generation X and Millennials are collaborative and comfortable with technology, Millennials are using networking and social media for information gathering and collaboration to give them an advantage as leaders. Millennial leaders exhibit the characteristics of their destiny as a *hero generation*[1] as demonstrated in the interview responses, describing the Millennial leaders' optimistic outlook on life and their passion to make the world a better place for others.

Millennial leaders described themselves as hands off, delegating, autonomous, passionate, motivating, and goal oriented. Many of these Millennial leaders were still uncertain of their leadership abilities, feeling that they were still learning or growing, and developing their skills or their style.

These leaders recognized that they are all still young and developing as leaders. They also recognized that experience is a component of good leadership. As Justin stated, "I'd say I'm still growing. I think in order to be a leader you have to have a lot of experience, and you have to endure any setbacks, any shortfalls." Millennial leaders who were interviewed defined leadership as inspiring others, being an example for others, being selfless, and looking out for the good of others. These Millennial leaders stated that they prefer leaders and role models who inspire them, act as examples for them, are selfless, and look out for the good of others.

Based on the results of the study, the self-described leadership style of Millennials meets the definition of servant leadership—leadership by one who wants to serve first, then aspires to lead.[2] Other key aspects of these Millennial leaders' leadership style are their collaborative nature, emphasis on networking, and social responsibility, which are congruent with the leader's ability to build relationships as a means to accomplish one's goals. These Millennial leaders have a strong relational component to their leadership, having developed team skills and the ability to work with others to achieve success together. As concluded by Jessica, "I think my last thoughts are creating more opportunities for leadership, our generation, taking advantage of the newer opportunities, stepping in, realizing the importance of having relationships with other people. Facebook does not suffice. We have to have real relationships."

Participants interviewed described themselves as passionate and discussed the importance of passion giving them the drive to want to lead others. The passionate, selfless, and collaborative nature of these Millennial leaders defines them and gives them their unique style.

Millennial leaders prefer leaders who are passionate and motivating, are visionary and can explain the goals, yet do not micromanage. At the same time, their preferred leaders are direct, provide constructive criticism, and are available when needed for support. These are all attributes the Millennial leaders mentioned as desirable, but did not claim to have mastered as part of their own leadership skills. These leaders strive to attain the skills they admire in others as they learn to delegate, motivate teams, and develop better communications skills.

Leadership development
for next-generation leaders

Most Millennial leaders are casual in their attitude and approach to work, collaborative and inclusive, and rely on technology, including social media, for access to information and networking with peers. Truth and integrity are important values to Millennial leaders, in addition to a desire for leaders to exhibit good moral values. Work-life balance and the relationship of work to family, friends, and volunteerism are also key concerns for the Millennial generation. Millennial leaders value the wisdom of experience and guidance from mentors. To be successful as leaders, they expect to have multiple mentors easily accessible and depend on their mentors for guidance. As Brandon described his relationship with mentors, "I have leaders in my life that are my advisors and mentors that I respect a lot and I interact with and interface with significantly, and what I expect out of them is what they expect out of me, which is to do the right thing." Millennial leaders do not like to be told how to do their work and prefer the freedom to learn by trial and error.

Their early leadership experiences, leadership training, observing negative examples, and learning from experience influenced Millennial leaders' leadership development. Early leadership experiences involved family, school, or sports situations where a family member, teacher, or coach had an impact on the individual view of a leader. According to Amber, "Becoming a leader is a constant training process. You have to identify the areas you need to develop, figure out the best ways to strengthen your weaknesses, and find mentors who will help you along the way." Although Millennials do not want to be told exactly how to do their jobs, they do appreciate the value of an experienced person telling them what has succeeded or failed in the past.

Millennial leaders compared to other generations

Millennial leaders believe they are different from leaders belonging to other generational groups. The descriptions that study participants gave when asked about their own leadership style or that of other Millennial leaders were used to update the comparisons of leadership styles from previous research, with data extracted from interviews to create a comparison table. Millennial leaders are driven by passion, whether that passion is for their vision, their organization, or helping others. Millennial leaders are more casual in their attitude and approach to work than previous generations. As leaders, Millennials prefer to be participative and share responsibility. Millennial leaders are more collaborative and inclusive, and rely more on technology, including social media, for access to information and peer networking. Millennial leaders want the opportunity to be creative and innovative. It is also important to these leaders to do the right thing, which invokes their values of family and friends first, work-life balance, and social responsibility.

Leadership Styles of Identified Generations Including Millennials

Generation	View of Trust as It Relates to Work
Traditionalists	Traditional, autocratic[3]; directive[4]; hierarchical[5]; command and control[6]
Baby Boomers	Democratic[7]; participative[8]; consensus building[9]; collegial, consensual, participative[10]
Generation X	Collaborative[11]; informed decision making[12]; competence[13]; challenging, information is power[14]; laissez-faire[15]
Millennials	Collaborative, inclusive, passionate, believe in doing the right thing, sharing responsibility, participative, casual, creative, innovative, rely on technology and social media for information and networking

Organizations will change as they recognize the need for mentoring programs for their future leaders. Training programs to meet the requirements for Millennial leaders' development need to be established within the organization or funded as external programs. The shifting view of leader from the Traditionalists' perspective as the top of the hierarchy holding the position that was earned by time on the job, to the Baby Boomer view of the position that was earned by consensus as the best person for the job, to the Generation X view that the leader was the most competent person, is now replaced by the Millennials' expectation that the leader is the best person to guide others.

Millennials' self-described leadership style

Millennial leaders are passionate about the causes they believe in, and they have to see that same passion in their organizations to want to be leaders in those organizations. Millennial leaders need to feel that they can trust their mentors, leaders, and the organizations to which they belong. Millennial leaders feel that people should be able to bring their talents together collaboratively and share in the knowledge needed to be successful. The leader is the person who can successfully inspire and drive the vision, not the person who keeps the knowledge. A good leader is looking out for others, whether that means on their team, in their organization, in the community, or for larger, global causes.

Millennial leaders have a strong view of leaders doing the right things. As leaders, Millennials feel they should do what is right and expect the same of other leaders. To the Millennial leader, the right thing is a clear message. Millennial leaders carry through with what they say they will do and expect others to do the same.

Millennial leaders realize they have a lot to learn and expect to continue learning. As part of learning to be good leaders, Millennials expect to be given opportunities to continue this learning process. Millennial leaders define leadership as inspiring others, being an example for others, being selfless, and looking out for the good of others.

Millennial leaders prefer leaders and role models who inspire others, act as an example for others, are selfless, and look out for the good of others. These leaders expect their role models to show humility and to have a desire to develop younger leaders by giving them guidance and sharing their experience.

This book provided discussions on the findings based on the responses to the interview questions and the analysis of the themes that evolved from the research questions. It provides new insight into the thoughts and feelings of Millennial leaders. It has the added perspective of an organizational leader who has management experience in a multigenerational workforce and has faced many of these issues as a manager, leader, and mentor of Millennials. Millennials will soon be the largest generational group in the workforce, so now is the time to take the opportunity to understand how these future leaders learn, communicate, interact with others, need to be recognized, and can be an asset to your organization.

Appendix

Study Participant Demographics

Participant characteristics	n ($N = 25$)
Age	
23	2
24	1
25	3
26	4
27	1
28	4
29	2
30	1
31	3
32	1
33	2
34	1

Type of employer

Business services	6
Education services	2
Financial/real estate	1
Government	4
Management consulting services	3
Marketing/advertising	1
Nonprofit	5
Media	3

Type of position held

Executive/management	11
Project manager/team lead	14

Bibliography

Introduction

1. Orrell, Lisa. "In economic crisis, think of the next generation." *Strategic Communication Management*, 2009, Vol. 13, 7.
2. Tulgan, Bruce. "Trends point to a dynamic generational shift in the future workforce." *Employment Relations Today*, 2004, Vol. 30, 23–31.
3. Orrell, Lisa. "In economic crisis, think of the next generation." *Strategic Communication Management*, 2009, Vol. 13, 7.

Chapter 1

1. Strauss, William and Neil Howe. *Generations: The History of America's Future, 1584 to 2069.* New York, NY: William Morrow, 1991.
2. Zemke, Ron, Claire Raines, and Bob Filipczak. *Generations at Work: Managing the Clash of Veterans, Boomers, Xers, and Nexters in Your Workplace.* New York, NY: AMA, 2000.
3. Hersey, Paul and Ken Blanchard. "So you want to know your leadership style?" *Training and Development Journal*, 1981, Vol. 35, No. 6, 34–48.
4. Social Security Administration. "Popular baby names by birth year." 2012. http://www.socialsecurity.gov/cgi-bin/popularnames.cgi.

Chapter 3

1. Kouzes, James M. and Barry Z. Posner. *The Leadership Challenge.* 4th ed. San Francisco, CA: Jossey-Bass, 2007.

2. Goleman, Daniel. *Emotional Intelligence: Why It Can Matter More Than IQ.* New York, NY: Bantam Books, 1995.

3. Kouzes, James M. and Barry Z. Posner. *The Leadership Challenge.* 4th ed. San Francisco, CA: Jossey-Bass, 2007.

4. Allio, Ron. "Bad leaders: How they get that way and what to do about them." *Strategy & Leadership,* 2007, Vol. 35, No. 3, 12–17. doi:10.1108/108785 70710745785.

5. Herman, Roger E. "A leadership evolution." *Employment Relations Today,* Winter 2000, Vol. 26, No. 4, 73–82.

6. Raines, Claire. *Connecting Generations: The Sourcebook for a New Workplace.* San Francisco, CA: Thompson Crisp Learning, 2003.

7. Lancaster, Lynn C. and David Stillman. *When Generations Collide: Who They Are. Why They Clash. How to Solve the Generational Puzzle at Work.* New York, NY: Harper Collins, 2002.

8. Ibid.

9. Sessa, Valerie I., Robert I. Kabacoff, Jennifer Deal, and Heather Brown. "Generational differences in leader values and leadership behaviors." *Psychologist-Manager Journal,* 2007, Vol. 10, No. 1, 47–74.

Chapter 4

1. TOMS Shoes. "Bio of Blake Mycoskie." www.toms.com/blakes-bio. n.d.

2. Schwarzenegger, Katherine. *I Just Graduated . . . Now What? Honest Answers from Those Who Have Been There.* New York, NY: Crown Archetype, 2014.

Chapter 6

1. Green, Daryl D. "Leading a postmodern workforce." *Academy of Strategic Management Journal*, 2007, Vol. 6, 15–26.
2. Ranier, Thom S. and Jess W. Ranier. *The Millennials: Connecting to America's Largest Generation*. Nashville, TN: B&H, 2011.
3. Fore, Carolyn W. "Next generation leadership: Millennials as leaders." PhD diss., Capella University, 2012. UMI No. 3553334.
4. Ryan, Rebecca. *Live First, Work Second: Getting inside the Head of the Next Generation*. Madison, WI: Next Generation Consulting, 2007.
5. Zemke, Ron, Claire Raines, and Bob Filipczak. *Generations at Work: Managing the Clash of Veterans, Boomers, Xers, and Nexters in Your Workplace*. New York, NY: AMA, 2000.
6. Ibid.

Chapter 7

1. Glass, Amy. "Understanding generational differences for competitive success." *Industrial and Commercial Training*, 2007, Vol. 39, No. 2, 98–103. doi:10.1108/00197850710732424.
2. Elam, Carol, Terry Stratton, and Denise D. Gibson. "Welcoming a new generation to college: The millennial students." *Journal of College Admission*, Spring 2007, No. 195, 20–25.
3. Glass, Amy. "Understanding generational differences for competitive success." *Industrial and Commercial Training*, 2007, Vol. 39, No. 2, 98–103. doi:10.1108/00197850710732424.
4. Tapscott, Don. *Grown Up Digital: How the Net Generation Is Changing Your World*. New York, NY: McGraw-Hill, 2009.

Chapter 8

1. Meister, Jeanne C. and Karie Willyerd. "Mentoring Millennials." *Harvard Business Review*. May 2010.

Chapter 9

1. Ancona, Deborah. "Leadership capabilities: Exercise them to develop a signature style." *Leadership Excellence*, 2010, Vol. 27, No. 2, 5–6.

2. Goleman, Daniel. *Emotional Intelligence: Why It Can Matter More Than IQ*. New York, NY: Bantam Books, 1995.

Chapter 10

1. Coleman, John, Daniel Gulati, and W. Oliver Segovia. *Passion and Purpose: Stories from the Best and Brightest Young Business Leaders*. Boston, MA: Harvard Business School, 2012.

Conclusion

1. Howe, Neil and William Strauss. *Millennials Rising: The Next Great Generation*. New York, NY: Random House, 2000.

2. Greenleaf, Robert. *Servant Leadership: A Journey into the Nature of Legitimate Power and Greatness*. Mahwah, NJ: Paulist Press, 1977.

3. Deegan, David. "The changing face of leadership: Past, present and future." *Training Journal*, December 2009, 45–48.

4. Salahuddin, Mecca M. "Generational differences impact on leadership style and organizational success." *Journal of Diversity Management*, Second Quarter 2010, Vol. 5, No. 2, 1–6.

5. Arsenault, Paul M. "Validating generational differences: A legitimate diversity and leadership issue." *Leadership & Organization Development Journal*,

2004, Vol. 25, No. 1/2, 124–141. doi:10.1108/0143 7730410521813.

6. Zemke, Ron, Claire Raines, and Bob Filipczak. *Generations at Work: Managing the Clash of Veterans, Boomers, Xers, and Nexters in Your Workplace.* New York, NY: AMA, 2000.

7. Deegan, David. "The changing face of leadership: Past, present and future." *Training Journal,* December 2009, 45–48.

8. Salahuddin, Mecca M. "Generational differences impact on leadership style and organizational success." *Journal of Diversity Management,* Second Quarter 2010, Vol. 5, No. 2, 1–6.

9. Crumpacker, Martha and Jill Crumpacker. "Succession planning and generational stereotypes: Should HR consider age-based values and attitudes a relevant factor or a passing fad?" *Public Personnel Management,* 2007, Vol. 36, No. 4, 349–369.

10. Zemke, Ron, Claire Raines, and Bob Filipczak. *Generations at Work: Managing the Clash of Veterans, Boomers, Xers, and Nexters in Your Workplace.* New York, NY: AMA, 2000.

11. Deegan, David. "The changing face of leadership: Past, present and future." *Training Journal,* December 2009, 45–48.

12. Salahuddin, Mecca M. "Generational differences impact on leadership style and organizational success." *Journal of Diversity Management,* Second Quarter 2010, Vol. 5, No. 2, 1–6.

13. Green, Daryl D. "Leading a postmodern workforce." *Academy of Strategic Management Journal,* 2007, Vol. 6, 15–26.

14. Zemke, Ron, Claire Raines, and Bob Filipczak. *Generations at Work: Managing the Clash of Veterans,*

Boomers, Xers, and Nexters in Your Workplace. New York, NY: AMA, 2000.

15. Hackman, Michael Z. and Craig E. Johnson. *Leadership: A Communication Perspective.* 5th ed. Long Grove, IL: Waveland Press, 2009.

About the Author

Carolyn White Fore, PhD, has many years of leadership experience in a corporate environment with responsibility for multigenerational teams. During those years she saw firsthand the differences in the leadership styles of leaders from different generational groups. She wrote her doctoral dissertation on next-generation leadership, focusing on Millennials as leaders, and through her research explored how Millennial leaders describe leaders, leading, and what leadership means.

Carolyn now teaches MBA students and continues to explore the leadership style of Millennials and how this generation is changing organizations. She states that she often hears criticism of the Millennial generation for not appreciating what they have, not being willing to work hard, and not understanding what the older generations have done for them, along with other negative sentiments, and is quick to defend them for the positive virtues they bring to the workplace, pointing out a few facts in their favor. She finds the Millennials a positive generation with a promising future and looks forward to seeing how they perform as the next generation of leaders.

Carolyn has a bachelor of arts in chemistry from the University of North Carolina at Chapel Hill, a master of education in business data processing from the University of Georgia, and a doctor of philosophy in organization and management from Capella University.